MORE FOOD FROM YOUR GARDEN

BY

JACOB R. MITTLEIDER, LLD.

AGRICULTURAL CONSULTANT
LECTURER, LOMA LINDA UNIVERSITY

ILLUSTRATED BY
DON BERGGREN

WOODBRIDGE® PRESS
SANTA BARBARA, CALIFORNIA

1990

Revised Edition

Published and Distributed by

Woodbridge Press Publishing Company
Post Office Box 6189
Santa Barbara, California 93160

World Rights Reserved

Library of Congress Catalog Card Number: 82-70475

International Standard Book Number: 0-912800-72-0

Distributed Simultaneously in the United States and Canada

Printed in the United States of America.

Library of Congress Cataloging in Publication Data:

Mittleider, Jacob R.
  More food from your garden.

  1. Vegetable gardening. I. Title.

SB321.M65 635 82-70475
ISBN 0-912800-72-0 pbk.

MORE FOOD FROM YOUR GARDEN

DEDICATION

This book is dedicated to my family —

Mildred Mittleider, patient and supportive wife, tolerant and brave amid the frustration and uncertainty of life with an adventurous husband. Without her, success would not have been possible.

Douglas and Carol Dietrich, son-in-law and daughter, who encouraged me in the development of the first experimental models that stimulated this entire program; and who still inspire toward continuing refinement and perfecting.

Dr. James R. and Jeannie Wise, son-in-law and daughter, who also built and planted the early model gardens whose success was convincing evidence that millions could benefit from these extraordinarily productive techniques — if only they had the information.

To these, and others, who encouraged and motivated me to accomplish that in which I really believed, I gratefully dedicate this book.

—The Author

ACKNOWLEDGEMENTS

I wish to thank —

Willis J. Hackett, for his confidence and encouragement, for his belief in the methodology, and for the foreword he generously wrote for this book and for a previous book.

Lynn Gair, M.D., for loyalty and personal involvement in past years, helping to bring this program to success. Without his help there would never have been the opportunity to develop it, either abroad or in the United States.

D. L. Stoops, M.D., whose humanitarian nature led him to study the Mittleider program thoroughly as a means of helping hungry peoples, and then to promote it and encourage its development.

Don Berggren, the illustrator of this book. Without his outstanding talent it would not have been possible to prepare this work for mankind. It is a rare privilege to work with so talented a person who is also selfless and sensitive to human need.

—The Author

APPENDICES

A PREFACE

Three decades of almost constant study and research on food production problems in many parts of the world have long since convinced me that the most promising approach is a synthesis of the best features of several major methods of gardening.

Organic gardening emphasizes plant access to all available soil nutrients and microbial activity; conventional gardening emphasizes adequate fertilization and pest control; hydroponic gardening emphasizes high-density planting in a controlled environment.

But each of these methods, alone, has some limitations.

What I have been demonstrating in various countries is a bringing together of the best scientific knowledge and experience in each of these approaches. I believe that the results speak for themselves.

This book is a step-by-step guidebook to the use of my methods by the home gardener. If you have a rewarding gardening experience and it is due in part to the instructions given here, I shall be amply rewarded for the effort involved.

I would encourage the serious student of gardening to obtain a copy of a previous book, coauthored with Dr. Andrew N. Nelson, a gifted man whom I greatly admire. Its title is *Food for Everyone* and it may be obtained through the publisher of this book.

— The Author

FOREWORD

Abundant food now flourishing on once arid and unproductive land because of the skill and ingenuity of Jacob Mittleider is a source of great hope to the world's hungry peoples whose desperate cries have echoed around the world.

I have seen the lifeless eyes and the spindly, wobbling legs of children denied the balanced nutrition of an adequate food supply. Hungry children of war-torn countries have snatched food from my own hands.

Students of the future declare that the prospects for feeding the increasing millions of the 1980's are grim. Mittleider has the answer. He is dedicated to the task of meeting the nutritional needs of poverty-stricken populations wherever they are found.

Single-handedly, he has demonstrated from Alaska to California, from Fiji to Okinawa and Africa, that even the most unproductive soils can produce an abundance. In many instances his methods have doubled and tripled production on abandoned land.

This book, like *Food for Everyone,* the work coauthored by Jacob Mittleider and Dr. Andrew N. Nelson, will be hailed by many as a practical contribution to making food production more efficient.

Mittleider's demonstrations and institutes everywhere have proved that his method can be used by anyone, anywhere, to transform unproductive lands and greatly increase crop yields.

I hope that the publication of this book, *More Food From Your Garden,* will help dispel hunger and produce beautiful gardens where now only thorns and weeds are growing.

— Willis J. Hackett

Vice President
World Conference of Seventh-day Adventists
Advisory Chairman
Education and World Relief

Washington, D. C.

II

Jacob R. Mittleider

INTRODUCTION - NEW ABUNDANCE FOR HUNGRY PEOPLE

The "miracle" garden yields you may have been reading about lately are for real — and actually are the result of some fairly simple new applications of well-established agricultural principles.

Jacob R. Mittleider is the plant "magician" who has been in scores of countries these past few years turning people on to the thrills of unbelievable gardening success.

He has moved into food-problem areas of New Guinea, Africa, Bangladesh, Latin America, the U.S.A. — and has started a "food revolution" every time.

How about 30 tons of sweet potatoes where only 4 had previously been possible? or 6,000 pounds of rice where only 1,000 pounds were considered normal? or 100 tons of tomatoes compared with 20 before?

Experts say that with Mittleider's simple methods, this earth could feed nine times its present population — with no further agricultural knowledge. That's about 32 billion people!

These same simple methods — now presented for the first time in a popular book — can help you to feed your family more abundantly...with food grown more easily...in less space...with fewer gardening problems...than you ever thought possible.

The Mittleider Method can be used on any kind of ground — rocky, hilly, alkaline, clay, depleted; in any kind of climate — hot, moderate, cold; at any time of year — winter or summer.

If you are so inclined, this method can be used to attain complete economic self-sufficiency on less than half an acre of land!

Mittleider's university-sponsored demonstration program in New Guinea used poor land where only scrubby growth had previously been possible (above) and turned it into lush, productive gardens (below).

High Commissioner James B. Lampert (right) and University President Tetsuo Takara of Okinawa join Mittleider in examining young cauliflower that will produce 18 tons per acre — every 10 weeks — on rocky hillsides of the Ryukyu Islands.

Mittleider has proven repeatedly that his unique grow-box concept, with his simple, plastic greenhouse plan can produce enough food on even an eighth of an acre (5,000 square feet — a small city lot!) to feed a family plus enough to sell for living expenses.

Governments, universities, and mission organizations sponsor international Mittleider institutes in which people from many lands learn how to dramatically improve the amount and quality of food available.

Mittleider students are at work in India, Borneo, the U.S.A., Taiwan, Okinawa, Japan, Fiji, the Philippines, Samoa, New Guinea, Africa, Latin America — almost anywhere you could name...anywhere people are interested in food!

It has been commonplace for people who observe the Mittleider Method to speak in terms usually reserved for magic shows. "Astonishing...I couldn't believe my eyes...spectacular...a miracle...a marvel...amazing."

15

Struggling bean plants barely survive with conventional gardening methods (above) but burst into abundance on the very same plot with Mittleider methods.

Abandoned as "devil land" — totally useless until the Mittleider Method was applied — this plot now provides a good diet for college students, and surpluses to sell for additional school funds.

B.D. Lakshman, with huge agricultural holdings in Fiji, declared, "Ten thousand speeches could not have convinced me, but in less than two hours of demonstrations I am completely converted. It is nothing short of a miracle."

The then High Commissioner James B. Lampert of Okinawa, urged the people of the Ryukyus to observe "this unique opportunity to gain spectacular results from the very soil which, for centuries, has brought much discouragement."

Ambassador Takase Jiro of Japan praised the Mittleider approach as "an accurate and practical program of superb food production; a practical method of solving the problem of feeding the increasing populations of the world."

Willis J. Hackett, a general vice president of the Seventh-day Adventist world conference, with special emphasis on education and world relief programs, declared that the Mittleider program "has certainly paid off in New Guinea" where its abundant crops continue after many years to help support educational institutions and to provide more nourishing diets for the people.

Africa to the Arctic — searing heat, freezing cold cannot stop the amazing productivity of nature when provided with adequate nutrients, water, shelter.

Bob Ackeroid, senior agricultural officer in New Guinea, reported, "I think everyone in the Agricultural Department has been amazed at the results. The work has surprised us and shown what can be done in this country."

Loma Linda University (California) sponsored Mittleider on a 24-nation survey of food production problems, leading directly to the development of a series of institutes co-sponsored in some cases by host governments.

It is no wonder that such authorities look to the Mittleider program with great expectations. Where machinery is not readily available, where soil is poor, where weather and pests are destructive, Jacob Mittleider has shown that simple, ordinary people, using simple, ordinary hand tools, can actually out-produce heavy farm equipment and great outlays of capital!

Imagine the sense of dignity and self-respect that comes to a family when almost overnight their life can be changed from one of

This African land is producing many times its former yield with custom-made soil in Mittleider grow-boxes — 44 tons of cabbage per acre every 12 weeks!

poverty and hunger to one of health, good food, good income — self-sufficiency and pride!

This has actually happened to so many families in so many parts of the world that an Okinawan magazine was moved to describe Mittleider as "a man who can give hope to people throughout the world."

Because his simple methods have proved so eminently successful for so many people in so many countries, Mittleider is convinced that "hunger is no longer an agricultural problem; it is a human problem, a social problem." If politicians, educators, and interest groups can cooperate, he says, this world can feed an expanding population indefinitely.

In the meantime, the Mittleider method can certainly be a helping hand for you, your family, and your friends... in making gardening far more rewarding — and productive — than you ever thought gardening could be.

Mittleider grow-boxes can be used for large-scale production of garden crops — or, in ones and twos, for backyard family gardens — with the same productivity.

Can you imagine this concentration of luscious tomatoes in ordinary gardening? This Mittleider grow-box provides ideal soil conditions and adequate nutrition to support close planting and heavy bearing — more food in less space!

Rocky hillsides become productive farms with the grow-box technique. The boxes can be used on any kind of terrain, over any kind of soil — previously barren land can "blossom as the rose"!

Jacob R. Mittleider is an international agricultural consultant and lecturer, Loma Linda University, Loma Linda, California. His institute and lecture schedule is booked well ahead; but if you or your group would like to hear him, he may be contacted through the publisher of this book.

— Howard B. Weeks, Ph.D.

Santa Barbara, California

A Mittleider seminar group in Okinawa fills grow-boxes with custom-made soil — learning how to produce super yields where nothing would grow before.

One grow-box for the back yard or hundreds of them for a university demonstration farm — the same spectacular results are realized all over the world. Mittleider students cover a steep hillside with boxes.

Six thousand pounds of rice per acre on land that used to produce 800 to 1,200 pounds; 21,000 pounds of green beans and 28,000 pounds of sweet potatoes per acre on previously unusable land. That's why the Mittleider Method is called a "food revolution" in many countries.

Crowds gather in the city to see the simple Mittleider grow-boxes and super-simple greenhouse-covering demonstrated as a means toward more self-reliance in home food production.

Name it and you can plant it in your grow-box — tender bell peppers, melons of all kinds; in high concentrations with high yields, for the greatest amount of food possible in whatever space you have to use.

THE MITTLEIDER
METHOD

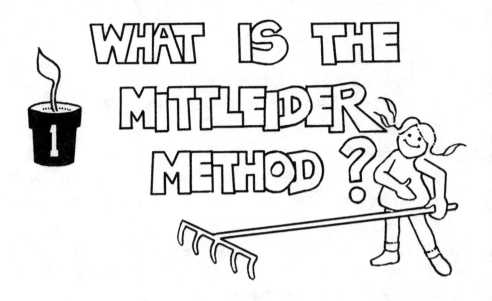

WHAT IS THE MITTLEIDER METHOD?

THE MITTLEIDER METHOD COMBINES THE BEST FEATURES OF SOIL GARDENING AND HYDROPONIC GARDENING. IT IS A COMPLETE, EASY-TO-FOLLOW PLAN THAT ELIMINATES GUESSWORK AND INSURES SUCCESS ANYWHERE; AN APARTMENT PATIO, A CITY YARD, A COUNTRY LOT, A FARM.

THE METHOD IS BASED ON MAXIMUM UTILIZATION OF SPACE, TIME, AND RESOURCES. CROPS ARE LARGE BECAUSE PLANTS ARE CLOSE TOGETHER, NOURISHED BY SUPPLEMENTAL FEEDINGS OF MINERAL NUTRIENTS, AS IN HYDROPONICS, BUT WITH NO SPECIAL EQUIPMENT.

UNLIKE HYDROPONICS, THE MITTLEIDER METHOD ALSO GIVES PLANTS ACCESS TO THE NATURAL SOIL FOR NUTRIENTS AS YET UNKNOWN OR THAT, WHILE NOT ESSENTIAL TO PLANT GROWTH, ARE USEFUL IN HUMAN NUTRITION.

TIME IS BETTER UTILIZED BECAUSE THE MITTLEIDER GROW-BOX AND SIMPLE GREENHOUSE GREATLY EXTEND THE GROWING SEASON. IN THE MITTLEIDER METHOD YOU HAVE A CLEAR PATTERN TO FOLLOW FOR SOIL PREPARATION, SEEDING AND PLANTING, FEEDING AND WATERING, PLANT CARE AND HARVESTING, AND PROTECTION FROM INSECTS, DISEASE, AND WEATHER. YOU SIMPLY CANNOT FAIL ___YOU WILL HAVE A SUCCESSFUL GARDEN IF YOU FOLLOW THE METHOD PRESENTED IN THIS BOOK.

HERE ARE SOME SPECIAL FEATURES OF THE MITTLEIDER METHOD:

1. "CUSTOM-MADE SOIL"

IN OPEN-FURROW GARDENING OR FARMING, MITTLEIDER PLANT NUTRITION COMPENSATES FOR NATURAL SOIL DEFICIENCIES. IN GROW-BOXES, SOIL CAN BE "CUSTOM-MADE" BY COMBINING NUTRIENTS WITH INERT AND ORGANIC MATERIALS LIKE SAND AND SAWDUST. (CHAPTER 4)

2. SIMPLE, GARDEN GROW-BOXES

OPEN, WOOD FRAMES, FILLED WITH "CUSTOM-MADE SOIL", PROVIDE FOR CONCENTRATED FOOD PRODUCTION IN LIMITED SPACE OR ON DIFFICULT TERRAIN, WITH NO SPECIAL EQUIPMENT OF ANY KIND. THE BOXES ALSO EXTEND THE GROWING SEASON AND SIMPLIFY THE "WORK" OF GARDENING. (CHAPTER 3)

3. PROVEN PLANT NUTRITION

THE MITTLEIDER NUTRIENT FORMULAS___ GIVEN TO
YOU IN THIS BOOK___ HAVE GREAT VALUE ;
THE RESULT OF 30 YEARS OF EXPERIENCE IN
ALMOST EVERY PART OF THE WORLD. THEY TAKE
THE GUESSWORK OUT OF PLANT FEEDING.
(CHAPTER 7 ; APPENDIX II)

4. SYSTEMATIC WATERING

THE MITTLEIDER METHOD USES 40 PERCENT
LESS WATER THAN DOES CONVENTIONAL
GARDENING. AT THE SAME TIME IT GIVES THIRSTY
PLANTS THE WATER THEY NEED MORE
CONSISTENTLY AND EFFECTIVELY. (CHAPTER 7)

5. PRODUCTIVE PLANT CARE

STEP-BY-STEP INSTRUCTIONS ARE GIVEN IN THIS
BOOK FOR TRAINING, PRUNING, POLLINATING,
PROTECTING PLANTS FROM INSECTS AND
DISEASE --- LETTING NATURE OUTDO HERSELF
IN PRODUCING ABUNDANT FOOD. (CHAPTERS 8,11)

6. PROTECTION FROM WEATHER

GREENHOUSE SHELTER BECOMES SIMPLE AND
INEXPENSIVE THE MITTLEIDER WAY. GROW-BOXES
CAN BE SIMPLY COVERED, GREENHOUSES SIMPLY
CONSTRUCTED. YOUR GROWING SEASON CAN BE
LONG AND PRODUCTIVE --- AT SMALL COST AND
WITH THE MOST ELEMENTARY EQUIPMENT.
(CHAPTERS 9,10,12)

WITH THE MITTLEIDER METHOD

1. ORDINARY PEOPLE CAN DO EXTRAORDINARY GARDENING.
2. SIMPLE, HAND LABOR CAN OUTPERFORM EXPENSIVE EQUIPMENT.
3. ABUNDANT FOOD CAN BE PRODUCED ON ANY KIND OF LAND, ON LESS LAND --- ANYWHERE IN THE WORLD.
4. SUCCESS IS CERTAIN BECAUSE NOTHING IS LEFT TO CHANCE.

J. R. Mittleider and his chief associate, Edmond Henkin (left), examine the produce of lush experimental and teaching gardens.

The Mittleider method makes the most of land area available by close spacing of plants in simple "grow-boxes," filled with inert or organic materials at hand plus nutrients.

It is like hydroponics in that supplemental feeding of nutrients make this close spacing highly productive; but unlike it in providing for root access to the natural soil for the best possible plant nutrition.

Simple greenhouse shelter, where necessary, produces abundant, year-round yields.

The Mittleider "grow-box" technique makes a real difference in home gardening. In the open or sheltered by a simple greenhouse covering, grow-boxes produce quality foods — to spare!

The best features of organic, hydroponic, and regular gardening produce outstanding quality in the Mittleider Method

Corn and tomatoes, cabbage and
potatoes, broccoli and onions,
melons, squash, and cucumbers —
or papaya and rice — name it and
you can grow it the Mittleider way!

Nitrogen

Potassium

Potassium

Symptoms of nutritional deficiencies. You no longer need to leave plants to the mercy of depleted or hostile soils. The Mittleider nutritional program will prevent most deficiencies and provides help should they appear. See Appendix III for description of symptoms and corrective measures.

Calcium

Boron

Molybdenum

2 GARDEN GROW BOXES
... MORE FOOD IN LESS SPACE ...

GROW-BOXES ARE BOTTOMLESS, WOODEN OR CEMENT FRAMES LEVELED IN PLACE. USUALLY 5 FEET WIDE, 30 FEET LONG, 8 INCHES DEEP; BUT THEY CAN BE ANY SIZE. THEY CAN BE BUILT ALMOST ANYWHERE. THEY ARE FILLED WITH "CUSTOM-MADE SOIL," A MIXTURE OF SAWDUST AND SAND, OR OTHER INERT AND ORGANIC COMBINATIONS TOGETHER WITH A BALANCE OF FERTILIZERS.

"CUSTOM-MADE SOIL" WITH ITS BALANCED NUTRIENTS AND PROPER MOISTURE AND FEEDING PRODUCE HIGHER YIELDS AND QUALITY ON MUCH LESS SPACE THAN REGULAR SOIL.

33

THE SOFT, "CUSTOM-MADE SOIL"
OFFERS MANY ADVANTAGES, INCLUDING
PERFECT DRAINAGE, AERATION, AND
BALANCED FEEDING. IT KEEPS
THE USUALLY HARD SUBSOIL
DAMP AND SOFT. THIS LETS
THE ROOTS PENETRATE THE
SUBSOIL AND ABSORB MANY
EXTRA IMPORTANT MINERALS.
THE GROWING SEASON IS LENGTHENED
BECAUSE IT HAS A COOLING EFFECT
ON ROOTS DURING THE HOT SUMMER AND BECAUSE
IT WARMS UP QUICKLY IN THE EARLY SPRING.
LEVEL GROW-BOXES FILLED WITH SOFT,
"CUSTOM-MADE SOIL" SAVE ABOUT 40 PERCENT IN
WATER; WATER PENETRATES UNIFORMLY, EASILY,
AND QUICKLY.

THE GROW-BOX MUST HAVE GOOD
DRAINAGE ALL AROUND THE FRAME.

A SPECIAL REASON FOR GROWING PLANTS IN
GROW-BOXES IS THAT YOU CAN CARE FOR THE CROP FROM
THE SIDES. SHOES CARRY DISEASE AND WEED SEEDS.
DO NOT WALK IN THE GROW-BOXES!

GROW-BOX GARDENING REQUIRES
FEW TOOLS. THE SOFT, "CUSTOM-MADE
SOIL" CAN BE WORKED
WITH BASIC HAND TOOLS
OR JUST WITH THE HANDS.

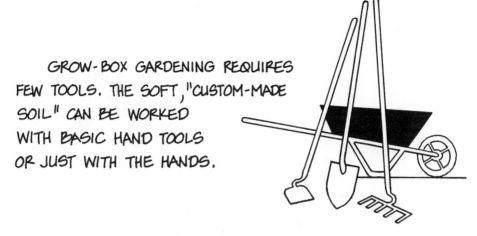

WITH GROW-BOXES YOU CAN MAKE GARDENS OF
ANY SIZE. FOUR GROW-BOXES CAN PROVIDE A NEARLY
CONTINUOUS HARVEST OF FOOD MUCH OF THE YEAR
FOR A FAMILY OF FOUR, IF PROPERLY MANAGED.
TEN GROW-BOXES CAN PROVIDE FOR A FAMILY'S
NEEDS AND A LARGE SURPLUS FOR SELLING OR
SHARING. TWENTY-FIVE TO FIFTY GROW-BOXES
CAN PROVIDE FOR COMPLETE ECONOMIC
SELF-SUFFICIENCY!

EVEN IN AREAS
WITH SEVERE WINTER
TEMPERATURES, THE GROW-BOXES
CAN BE COVERED EASILY TO MAKE INEXPENSIVE
GREENHOUSES AS SHOWN IN CHAPTER 9.

FOOD PRODUCED IN GROW-BOXES BY THE
MITTLEIDER METHOD IS EQUAL OR SUPERIOR
TO THAT GROWN BY ANY OTHER METHOD. IT
COMBINES THE BEST OF HYDROPONICS, ORGANIC,
AND CONVENTIONAL GARDENING METHODS.
IT EMPHASIZES THE USE OF BALANCED NUTRIENTS.
IT PROVIDES FOR ROOT ACCESS TO THE SOIL
UNDERNEATH THE BOXES. THE PLANTS THUS ABSORB
TRACES OF ALL OTHER AVAILABLE NUTRIENTS FOUND
IN MINERAL SOILS, NUTRIENTS VERY LIKELY
NEEDED BY MAN.

HOW TO MAKE GROW BOXES

3

SELECT A SUNNY LOCATION.
IN COOL CLIMATES, BUILD BOXES
WITH A SOUTHERN EXPOSURE NEAR
A HOUSE, PATIO, BARN OR DUG
INTO A HILLSIDE.

YOU CAN EVEN BUILD GROW-BOXES ON POOR,
HILLSIDE LAND, ROCKY SOIL, CLAY, ALKALI, OR ASPHALT.
IT DOESNT MATTER, THE GROW-BOXES WILL WORK!
JUST LEVEL OR TERRACE THE SPACE FOR THE
GROW-BOXES. PROVIDE GOOD DRAINAGE AWAY FROM
THE GROW-BOXES. ROOTS DROWN IN
STANDING WATER.

BUILD THE NUMBER OF GROW-BOXES NEEDED TO FIT YOUR PLOT. GROW-BOX SIZE CAN VARY TO FIT UNUSUAL BOUNDARIES. IF SEVERAL GROW-BOXES ARE BUILT SIDE-TO-SIDE, LINE THEM UP STRAIGHT FOR ATTRACTIVENESS AND EASY WORKING. PROVIDE 3'-0" OF WORKING SPACE ON EACH SIDE OF THE BOX AND 5'-0" OF WORKING SPACE AT THE ENDS OF THE BOX.

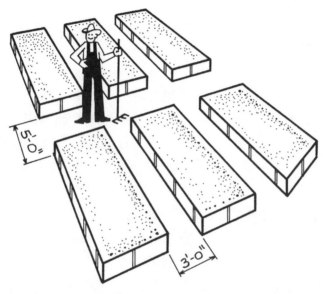

HERE IS THE MATERIALS LIST FOR THE STANDARD 5-FOOT-WIDE, 30-FOOT-LONG AND 8-INCH-DEEP MITTLEIDER GROW-BOX.

A) 70 FEET OF 1"x8" REDWOOD OR CEDAR.
B) 24 - 1"x2"x18"LONG POINTED REDWOOD STAKES.
C) ONE POUND OF 4" NAILS.
D) ONE THREE-POUND HAMMER OR MALL.
E) ONE REGULAR CLAW HAMMER.
F) 100 FEET OF STRONG CORD.
G) ONE LEVEL AT LEAST TWO FEET LONG.

HERE IS HOW TO BUILD
THE STANDARD 5'x30'x8"
MITTLEIDER GROW-BOX :

LEVEL ENOUGH GROUND FOR EACH BOX AREA.
ESTABLISH THE LOCATION OF THE CORNERS OF THE
GROW-BOX WITH THE CORD. TIE THE CORD
SECURELY TO THE STAKES.
NOTE: CORNERS SHOULD BE SQUARE (90°) UNLESS
THE AREA IS IRREGULAR IN SHAPE.

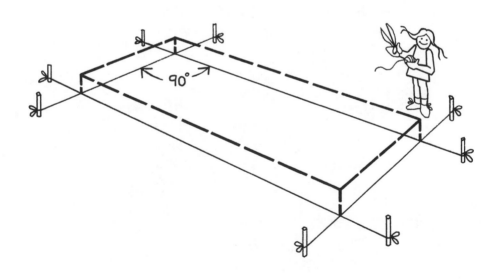

NINE INCHES FROM A CORNER, ALONG ONE SIDE, DRIVE THE FIRST STAKE INTO THE GROUND, TO A DEPTH OF ABOUT NINE INCHES. ALWAYS DRIVE STAKES ON THE OUTSIDE EDGES OF THE GROW-BOX, <u>NEVER</u> ON THE INSIDE EDGES. DRIVE STAKES ABOUT 30 INCHES APART ALONG THE CORD LINE FOR ONE SIDE OF THE BOX. WHEN NAILED SECURELY TO THE LEVELED 1"x8" BOARDS, THE TOP EDGES OF BOARDS AND THE STAKES SHOULD BE LEVEL (FLUSH).

NAIL A 1"x8" SIDE BOARD FLUSH WITH TOP OF STAKE NEAREST A BOX END. DRIVE STAKE AND SIDE BOARD DEEPER TOGETHER UNTIL BOTTOM EDGE OF SIDE BOARD TOUCHES THE GROUND. PROCEED TO SECOND STAKE.

40

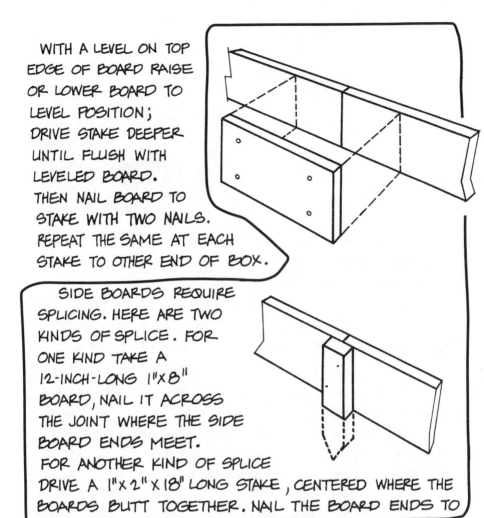

WITH A LEVEL ON TOP EDGE OF BOARD RAISE OR LOWER BOARD TO LEVEL POSITION; DRIVE STAKE DEEPER UNTIL FLUSH WITH LEVELED BOARD. THEN NAIL BOARD TO STAKE WITH TWO NAILS. REPEAT THE SAME AT EACH STAKE TO OTHER END OF BOX.

SIDE BOARDS REQUIRE SPLICING. HERE ARE TWO KINDS OF SPLICE. FOR ONE KIND TAKE A 12-INCH-LONG 1"x 8" BOARD, NAIL IT ACROSS THE JOINT WHERE THE SIDE BOARD ENDS MEET. FOR ANOTHER KIND OF SPLICE DRIVE A 1"x 2" x 18" LONG STAKE, CENTERED WHERE THE BOARDS BUTT TOGETHER. NAIL THE BOARD ENDS TO THE STAKE.

NAIL A 5-FOOT BOX END-PIECE (1"x 8") TO EACH END OF THE LEVELED SIDE.

DRIVE A STAKE NEAR THE
CENTER OF BOTH 5-FOOT BOX
ENDS IN LINE WITH THE CORD.
PLACE LEVEL LIKE A TRIANGLE ACROSS TOPS OF BOTH
SIDE AND END BOARDS. LEVEL THE 5-FOOT BOARD,
DRIVE STAKE TO PROPER DEPTH, AND NAIL TO 5-FOOT
END-PIECE. REPEAT THE SAME FOR OPPOSITE END OF BOX.

TO LEVEL THE OPPOSITE SIDE BOARD, PLACE LEVEL,
AGAIN LIKE A TRIANGLE, ACROSS THE 5-FOOT END-PIECE
AND THE TOP OF THE 1"x 8" SIDE BOARD. LEVEL SIDE
BOARD TO MATCH 5-FOOT END-PIECE. DRIVE STAKE
TO PROPER DEPTH, NAIL BOARD TO STAKE.

REPEAT, AS FOR FIRST
SIDE BOARD, AND CONTINUE
TO OPPOSITE END OF BOX.

42

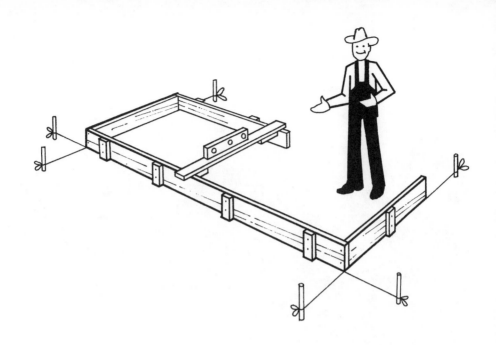

WHEN MANY GROW-BOXES ARE TO BE BUILT,
HERE IS A METHOD TO SPEED UP CONSTRUCTION.
STRETCH AND STAKE CORDS FOR THE TWO BOX ENDS
AND ONLY ONE SIDE. LEVEL THE SIDE ALONG THE CORD.
USE "SPREADER BOARD" AND THE LEVEL TO LEVEL THE
OTHER SIDE AND THE TWO ENDS.

NOTE "SPREADER BOARD" IS A 2"x4" X 6-FOOT-
LONG BOARD WITH 2"x4" X 6"-LONG BLOCKS NAILED
60 INCHES APART (OUTSIDE DIMENSION). THE TWO
BLOCKS CONTROL THE INSIDE WIDTH OF THE BOX.

PLACE THE SPREADER BOARD HORIZONTALLY ACROSS
THE BOX. BY RAISING OR LOWERING THE LOOSE SIDE
BOARDS TO THE LEVEL ON THE "SPREADER BOARD"
YOU CAN MAKE THE LOOSE SIDE LEVEL, LINE IT
UP STRAIGHT, STAKE, AND NAIL IT IN ONE
OPERATION!

43

Members of a Mittleider class and workshop clean up the area after construction of grow-boxes. The boxes are now ready to be filled with custom-made soil.

USING "CUSTOM·MADE" SOIL
4

"CUSTOM-MADE SOIL" IS USED TO AVOID CROP FAILURES. CROPS FAIL IN STUBBORN, HARD-TO-MANAGE SOILS BECAUSE OF SOIL DISEASE AND INSECTS, GOPHERS, MOLES, AND RABBITS. ALSO THERE IS THE CONSTANT BATTLE AGAINST WEEDS, AND THE NUTRIENT DEFICIENCIES IN SOILS WHICH ARE BECOMING MORE AND MORE SERIOUS. "CUSTOM-MADE SOIL" - THE HEART OF THE MITTLEIDER METHOD - IS USED TO AVOID ALL THESE DISAPPOINTMENTS. IT ASSURES SUCCESS EVERY TIME, AND GREATLY INCREASES YIELDS!

WHAT IS "CUSTOM·MADE SOIL"?

IT IS A MIXTURE OF INERT AND ORGANIC MATERIALS LIKE GRAVEL, SAND, SAWDUST, ETC., TO HOLD THE PLANTS - PLUS THE NUTRIENTS DESCRIBED IN THIS BOOK. IT PERFORMS ALL THE FUNCTONS OF AN IDEAL NATURAL SOIL. SOIL IS NO MYSTERY; IT IS SIMPLY TINY...SOMETIMES NOT SO TINY___ROCK FRAGMENTS, PLUS NUTRIENTS FROM VARIOUS SOURCES.

45

HERE'S HOW TO MAKE IT!
"CUSTOM-MADE SOIL" FOR SURE
GARDENING SUCCESS.

CHOOSE ANY AVAILABLE MATERIALS LIKE THESE AND
MAKE THE COMBINATION YOU LIKE BEST.

1. 50% BLOWSAND WITH 50% PEAT MOSS.
2. 75% SAWDUST WITH 25% FINE SAND.
3. 50% PERLITE WITH 50% PEAT MOSS OR SAWDUST.
4. 50% SAWDUST WITH 50% STYROFOAM PELLETS
   OR PIECES.

NOTE: BLOWSAND IS FINE SAND LIKE THAT HEAPED UP
BY THE WIND (SAND DUNES).

PERLITE IS BITS OF VOLCANIC GLASS "POPPED" BY HEAT.
IT IS AVAILABLE AT CONSTRUCTION SUPPLIERS.

SAWDUST IS SAFE TO USE FROM ALMOST ALL KINDS
OF WOOD. FRESH FROM THE SAW OR AGED - EITHER
IS GOOD. AVOID SHAVINGS. THEY ARE MISERABLE TO
MIX AND PLANT IN. THEY TEND TO FLATTEN INTO
LAYERS AND SOUR.

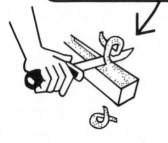

REMEMBER THE SOIL UNDER YOUR
GROW-BOX CAN BE SAND, ROCKS,
GRAVEL, GOOD SOIL, PEAT, CLAY,
OR CEMENT.

SPREAD TEN POUNDS GYPSUM (LIME) EVENLY
OVER THE INSIDE AREA OF ONE 5'x 30' GROW-BOX.
FILL THE GROW-BOX <u>LEVEL FULL</u> WITH THE MIXTURE
YOU CHOSE FROM THE FOUR
COMBINATIONS
LISTED EARLIER.
DO NOT TAMP OR
PACK THE SOIL
MIXTURE.

NOTE: OVER-FILLED
BOXES CANNOT BE
WATERED ACCURATELY.

MIX THE MATERIAL
THOROUGHLY. A RAKE
OR SMALL ROTOTILLER
WILL WORK NICELY.

WHILE MIXING, ADD
ENOUGH WATER TO
PRODUCE A WET MEDIUM, BUT NOT SO WET
YOU COULD SQUEEZE WATER FROM IT.

HERE ARE THE INGREDIENTS FOR THE MITTLEIDER PRE-PLANT FERTILIZER MIX. CAREFULLY WEIGH AND MIX TOGETHER THE FOLLOWING. IF NOT AVAILABLE AT YOUR GARDEN SUPPLY STORE, WRITE THE PUBLISHER FOR CURRENT SOURCES.

1. 4 POUNDS DOUBLE SUPERPHOSPHATE.
2. 2 POUNDS POTASSIUM SULFATE OR CHLORIDE.
3. 4 POUNDS SULFATE OF AMMONIA.
4. 2 POUNDS MAGNESIUM SULFATE.
5. <u>2 OUNCES</u> (60 GRAMS) BORON (SODIUM BORATE OR BORIC ACID).

SPREAD THIS DRY MIXTURE EVENLY OVER THE "CUSTOM-MADE SOIL" IN THE GROW-BOX. NOW SPREAD 5 POUNDS GYPSUM (LIME) EVENLY OVER THE GROW-BOX AREA RIGHT ON TOP OF THE OTHER FERTILIZERS.

NOTE: FOR <u>LIME</u>, USE GYPSUM IN ARID AREAS. USE AGRICULTURAL OR DOLOMITE LIME IN AREAS THAT GET MORE THAN 20 INCHES OF RAIN YEARLY.

THOROUGHLY MIX EVERYTHING IN THE
GROW-BOX TOGETHER - THE "CUSTOM-MADE SOIL",
LIME, AND PRE-PLANT FERTILIZERS. ADD ENOUGH
WATER TO MAKE A WET MIXTURE. <u>DO NOT</u> OVER-FILL
THE GROW-BOX WITH "SOIL" MIXTURE. FINISH BY
NEATLY LEVELING THE COMPLETE MIXTURE TO
THE TOP EDGE OF THE GROW-BOX. SPRINKLE
LIGHTLY, USING A FINE WATER SPRAY, TO KEEP
THE SOIL SURFACE FROM RAPID DRYING.

CONGRATULATIONS !!
YOUR GROW-BOX IS COMPLETE AND READY FOR
PLANTING. YOU CAN PLANT SEED DIRECTLY IN
THE BOX OR YOU CAN TRANSPLANT SEEDLINGS
FROM THE NURSERY OR FROM YOUR OWN
STARTING FRAMES.

HERE IS THE AMAZING THING YOU HAVE DONE IN THIS CHAPTER:

1. YOU HAVE CREATED A SPECIAL KIND OF SOIL AND PLACED IT IN A PROTECTIVE FRAME THAT WILL LET YOU ENJOY THE PLEASURES OF GARDENING WITHOUT ITS USUAL HEADACHES.

2. YOUR "SOIL" IS RICH AND EASY TO WORK. ROOTS CAN PENETRATE INTO THE PERPETUALLY MOIST SUBSOIL FOR ADDED, PERHAPS UNKNOWN NUTRIENTS.

3. EXPERIENCES AROUND THE WORLD SHOW THAT YOU CAN DOUBLE AND TRIPLE ORDINARY GARDEN YIELDS ANYWHERE, IN ANY CLIMATE.

4. WITH THIS SIMPLE PLAN YOU CAN GROW IN YOUR OWN YARD ALL THE PRODUCE YOU NEED. BY ADDING GROW-BOXES YOU CAN EVEN, IF YOU WISH, BECOME ECONOMICALLY SELF-SUFFICIENT ON AN ACRE OR LESS.

PLANNING YOUR GARDEN LAYOUT

YOUR GROW-BOX IS READY TO PLANT. EASY TO WORK, IN A SMALL SPACE--AND IT WILL PRODUCE MORE DELICIOUS, HEALTHFUL FOOD THAN YOU EVER IMAGINED.

WHAT CAN YOU PLANT?

NAME IT AND YOU CAN PLANT IT IN A MITTLEIDER GROW-BOX :

GREEN BEANS	HERBS
TOMATOES	CELERY
PEPPERS	PEANUTS
MELONS	
ZUCCHINI	
BROCCOLI	
CUCUMBERS	PEAS
CAULIFLOWER	BEETS
CABBAGE	SPINACH
RADISHES	POTATOES
EGGPLANT	ONIONS
CHARD	PARSLEY

51

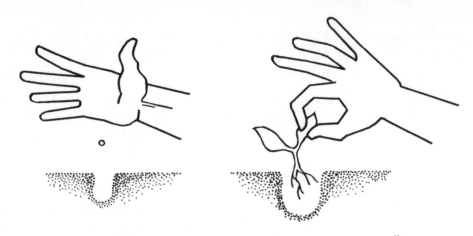

SEED DIRECTLY INTO THE "CUSTOM-MADE SOIL" IN THE
GROW-BOX (SEE CHAPTER 6), OR TRANSPLANT YOUNG
SEEDLINGS. YOU CAN PICK FRESH PRODUCE 8 TO 12 WEEKS
EARLIER BY TRANSPLANTING SEEDLINGS. GROW YOUR
OWN SEEDLINGS FOLLOWING THE MITTLEIDER METHOD
SHOWN IN CHAPTER 13, OR GET THEM FROM YOUR
GARDEN SHOP.

THE GROW-BOXES ADD EXTRA DAYS TO THE
GROWING SEASON. EARLY, FROSTY NIGHTS KILL
SOME CROPS, BUT HERE IS A LIST OF SOME WHICH
CAN BE PLANTED EVEN THEN. IF MATURE ENOUGH,
THEY CAN REMAIN IN THE GARDEN UNTIL MID-DECEMBER
IF PROTECTED BY SNOW, LEAVES, OR STRAW.

HERE IS A LIST SHOWING THE LATEST DESIRABLE
DATES FOR PLANTING SOME COMMON CROPS.
(SEED IN MOST CASES, TRANSPLANT IN OTHERS.)

MAY 15 .... TOMATOES , PEPPERS

JULY 1 .... CORN , ZUCCHINI
JULY 5 .... POTATOES
JULY 10 .... COLLARDS
JULY 15 .... GREEN BEANS , BEETS

AUGUST 1 .... CARROTS , ONIONS , GARLIC ,
                CAULIFLOWER
AUGUST 10 .... KALE
AUGUST 15 ...... BROCCOLI , CHARD ,
                BRUSSEL SPROUTS , CABBAGE
AUGUST 10 → 20 ...... RUTABAGAS
AUGUST 20 ...... LETTUCE

SEPTEMBER 1 .... TURNIPS
SEPTEMBER 10 .... SPINACH , MUSTARD GREENS
                CELERY

OCTOBER 1 ..... RADISHES

DATES ARE BASED ON CLIMATE IN THE
PACIFIC NORTHWEST. ALL EXCEPT THOSE
LISTED IN MAY AND JULY WILL WITHSTAND
10-DEGREE TEMPERATURES, ZERO IF
PROTECTED BY SNOW OR STRAW.

HERE IS A SAMPLE PLANTING LAYOUT. IT HAS TASTE APPEAL AND VARIETY FOR YOUR TABLE, LASTING FOR MONTHS.

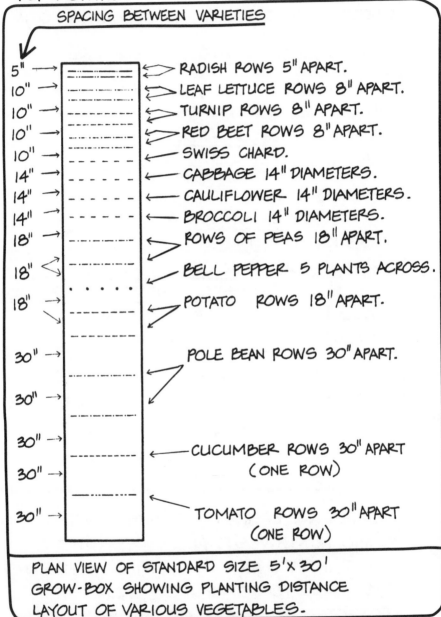

SPACING BETWEEN VARIETIES

5" → RADISH ROWS 5" APART.
10" → LEAF LETTUCE ROWS 8" APART.
10" → TURNIP ROWS 8" APART.
10" → RED BEET ROWS 8" APART.
10" → SWISS CHARD.
14" → CABBAGE 14" DIAMETERS.
14" → CAULIFLOWER 14" DIAMETERS.
14" → BROCCOLI 14" DIAMETERS.
18" → ROWS OF PEAS 18" APART.
18" → BELL PEPPER 5 PLANTS ACROSS.
18" → POTATO ROWS 18" APART.
30" → POLE BEAN ROWS 30" APART.
30" →
30" → CUCUMBER ROWS 30" APART (ONE ROW)
30" →
30" → TOMATO ROWS 30" APART (ONE ROW)

PLAN VIEW OF STANDARD SIZE 5' x 30' GROW-BOX SHOWING PLANTING DISTANCE LAYOUT OF VARIOUS VEGETABLES.

AFTER A CROP IS HARVESTED, IMMEDIATELY APPLY THE MITTLEIDER PRE-PLANT FERTILIZER MIX AGAIN (CHAPTER 4). MIX AND REPLANT THE SAME VARIETY OR A DIFFERENT CROP.

54

SHADE RUINS SOME CROPS. PLANT TALL GROWERS
ON THE NORTH SIDE OF THE LOW-GROWING CROPS.
TO STRETCH THE TABLE SUPPLY OF FRESH VEGETABLES
SCHEDULE TEN DAYS BETWEEN PLANTINGS OF
RADISHES, CARROTS, TURNIPS, LEAF LETTUCE,
BEETS, ETC.

PROPER SPACING GIVES PLANTS LIVING SPACE
TO GROW. THE GROW-BOXES ALLOW MORE PLANTS
TO GROW, AND GROW BETTER IN A SMALLER SPACE.
THIS IS POSSIBLE BECAUSE YOU ARE BRINGING MORE OF
THE NUTRIENTS TO THE PLANT. ROOTS DO NOT NEED
AS MUCH ROOM TO ROAM. BELOW IS A MARKER FOR
UNIFORM PLANT SPACING. IT IS A 1"x 2" x 5' BOARD
WITH ½" DIAMETER x 2½" LONG WOOD DOWELS SET
AT 7" OR 14" SPACINGS.

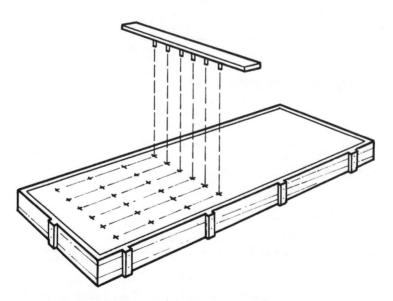

THE MARKER IS IMPORTANT; IT ASSURES EACH
PLANT ITS PROPER SPACING. THE TOOL IS USED TO
MARK BOTH THE LENGTH AND WIDTH OF THE GROW-BOX.

HERE IS A LIST OF PLANTS AND
SPACING RECOMMENDATIONS.

	DISTANCE BETWEEN INDIVIDUAL SEEDS AND PLANTS.	DISTANCE BETWEEN ROWS OF PLANTS.
CARROTS, TURNIPS	SEED LIGHTLY IN ROWS	7"
GREEN ONIONS	VERY CLOSE TOGETHER	4"
RADISHES	1"	5"
PEAS, SOYBEANS	1"	18"
BEETS	2"	5"
ONIONS	2"	6"
BUSH BEANS	2"	18"
SQUASH, EGGPLANT	3 PLANTS ACROSS THE 5' WIDE GROW-BOX	28"
PEANUTS	4"	18"
POLE BEANS	5"	24"
SPINACH	7"	10"
BELL PEPPERS, CORN	7"	18"
CUCUMBERS, TOMATOES	7"	48"
POTATOES	10"	14"
SWEET POTATOES	12"	18"
CABBAGE, HEAD LETTUCE, CAULIFLOWER, CELERY, BROCCOLI	14"	14"
LEAF LETTUCE	2"	8"

MAKE YOUR GARDEN ATTRACTIVE. IT IS PRACTICAL, MAGNETIC, AND A SOURCE OF PLEASURE AND PRIDE! GROW ONE CROP IN YOUR GROW-BOX, IF YOU CHOOSE, OR GROW A VARIETY.

PLANTING YOUR GARDEN GROW BOX

6

YOU CAN SOW SEEDS DIRECTLY, OR YOU CAN TRANSPLANT PLANTS INTO YOUR GROW-BOXES. IF YOU SOW SEEDS DIRECTLY INTO YOUR GROW-BOX REMEMBER THESE POINTS:

1. USE CERTIFIED SEED, WHENEVER POSSIBLE. (CERTIFIED SEED IS PRODUCED UNDER MORE RIGID INSPECTION.)
2. BE SURE THE SOIL MIXTURE AND THE SOIL SURFACE IN THE GROW-BOX ARE WET, NOT JUST DAMP.
3. DON'T PLANT TOO EARLY WHILE THE SOIL IS COLD!
4. DO NOT COVER SEEDS DEEP. USE THE FOLLOWING AS A GUIDE.

COVER SEEDS 2½ TIMES THEIR THICKNESS (NOT THEIR LENGTH).

SEEDS THE SIZE OF PEAS, BEANS, PEANUTS – THREE TO FOUR TIMES THEIR THICKNESS.

57

DO NOT COVER SMALL SEEDS LIKE PARSLEY,
DILL, OR CARROTS WITH SOIL. A GENTLE
WATERING AFTER SOWING GIVES ADEQUATE
COVERING. YOU WILL HAVE MORE SUCCESS
IN GERMINATING SMALL SEEDS IF, AFTER
SOWING AND GENTLY WATERING, YOU COVER
THEM WITH A LAYER OF BURLAP OR CHEESE CLOTH.
GENTLY WATER THROUGH THIS COVERING UNTIL
THE SEEDS BEGIN SPROUTING.

REMOVE THE BURLAP COVERING AS SOON
AS YOU SEE THE FIRST WHITE SEED-SPROUT.
FAILURE TO DO THIS WILL RESULT IN WEAK, THIN
SEEDLINGS. SEEDLINGS REQUIRE LOTS OF
LIGHT QUICKLY.

TRANSPLANTING YOUNG SEEDLINGS

YOU CAN REALIZE EARLIER PRODUCE AND HARVEST
BIGGER CROPS BY TRANSPLANTING HEALTHY
SEEDLINGS PURCHASED FROM THE NURSERY OR
GARDEN SHOP, OR GROWING THEM YOURSELF
IN SEED-STARTING BOXES. (SEE CHAPTER 13).
ONE OF THE "MOST FUN" PARTS OF GARDENING IS
TRANSPLANTING STRONG, HEALTHY SEEDLINGS !

NOTE: YOUNG SEEDLINGS NEED PROTECTION
FROM PESTS. ESPECIALLY CUTWORMS, SNAILS,
SLUGS AND SOIL MAGGOTS. POISONED BAIT OR
PELLETS CAN BE PURCHASED FROM YOUR
GARDEN SUPPLY STORE. FOLLOW DIRECTIONS
CAREFULLY.

FOLLOW THESE RULES FOR GREATEST SUCCESS

1. CHECK THE PRE-PLANT FERTILIZER MIX. IF THESE NUTRIENTS HAVEN'T BEEN SPREAD ON THE "SOIL" MIXTURE IN THE GROW-BOX, DO IT NOW. (SEE CHAPTER 4)

2. REPLENISH THE MOISTURE SUPPLY IN THE GROW-BOX BY WATERING FAIRLY HEAVILY THE AFTERNOON BEFORE YOU PLANT.

3. THE NEXT MORNING, THOROUGHLY STIR, MIX, AND LOOSEN THE "SOIL" MIXTURE. THIS CAN BE DONE QUICKLY AND EASILY WITH A 4-TINED CURVED FORK, GARDEN RAKE, OR ROTOTILLER.

4. WITHOUT ANY DELAY, RAKE AND LEVEL THE "SOIL" MIXTURE EVEN AND SMOOTH.

5. IMMEDIATELY GIVE THE "SOIL" A LIGHT SPRINKLING TO KEEP THE SURFACE FROM DRYING TOO MUCH. BE SURE THE GROW-BOX IS LEVEL-FULL WITH THE "SOIL" MIXTURE.

6. THE GROW-BOX SURFACE AREA IS NOW READY TO BE MARKED WITH THE MARKER TO PROVIDE EACH PLANT WITH THE SPACING AND GROWING AREA IT MUST HAVE.

Healthy young seedlings off to a good start in a Mittleider grow-box filled with nutrient-rich, custom-made soil.

GENTLY REMOVE A PLANT
FROM THE SEED BOX (FLAT)
BY LOOSENING THE ROOTS
WITH TWO FINGERS WHILE
LIFTING THE PLANT BY
THE SEED LEAF WITH
THE OTHER HAND.
ALWAYS HANDLE PLANTS
BY THEIR LEAVES.

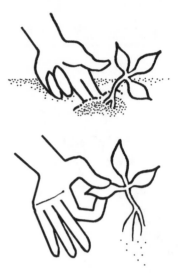

TRANSPLANT IN THREE MOTIONS

1. WITH THE LEFT HAND
MAKE (SHAPE) THE <u>PROPER</u>
SIZE HOLE, IN ONE
BACKWARD PULLING
MOTION. (DO NOT MOVE
HAND FROM HOLE.)

NOTE : A PROPER SIZE HOLE IS LARGE
ENOUGH FOR THE ROOTS OF THE PLANT TO
CLEAR WITHOUT CURLING OR TURNING UP FROM
BRUSHING AGAINST THE SIDES OF THE HOLE.

2. GENTLY LOWER
   PLANT (HELD IN
   RIGHT HAND) INTO
   THE HOLE TO THE
   PROPER DEPTH.

NOTE: THE PROPER DEPTH WILL ALLOW
THE PLANT TO STAND WITHOUT TIPPING
OVER, OR BE BLOWN OUT OF THE "SOIL"
BY LIGHT WINDS.

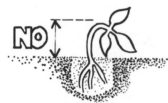

3. REMOVE THE LEFT HAND FROM THE HOLE
   AND IN THE SAME MOTION PRESS
   (ONCE ONLY) THE SOIL FIRMLY (BUT NOT
   SEVERELY) AGAINST THE PLANT ROOTS.
   DO NOT PACK OR PAT THE SOIL AROUND
   THE PLANT.

TO HELP REDUCE THE
SHOCK OF TRANSPLANTING
QUICKLY POUR AROUND
EACH PLANT ONE PINT OF
A TRANSPLANTING SOLUTION
(FUNGICIDE AND DRENCH
INCLUDED IF NECESSARY).

TRANSPLANTING SOLUTION
A FIVE-GALLON BATCH WILL TREAT
              40 PLANTS
  5 GALLONS OF WATER
  2¼ OUNCES AMMONIUM NITRATE
  1½ OUNCES DIAMMONIUM PHOSPHATE
  20 GRAMS POTASSIUM SULFATE OR CHLORIDE
  20 GRAMS MAGNESIUM SULFATE (EPSOM SALT)

NOTE: IF FUNGUS DISEASES ARE PRESENT
(ESPECIALLY IN TROPICAL AREAS) ADD
35 GRAMS OF A GOOD FUNGICIDE POWDER.
LOCAL AGRICULTURAL OFFICERS CAN HELP YOU
IDENTIFY DISEASE PROBLEMS.

TO CONTROL "WHIPTAIL DISEASE" CAUSED BY
MOLYBDENUM DEFICIENCY ADD 20 GRAINS
(NOT GRAMS) SODIUM MOLYBDATE OR
MOLYBDIC ACID. TO CONTROL SOIL MAGGOTS
ADD 20 GRAMS DIAZINON POWDER
(OR SOME SIMILAR PRODUCT).

ALL THESE MATERIALS CAN BE ADDED AND
APPLIED IN ONE OPERATION.
USE CHEMICALS ONLY WHEN REQUIRED.
BE VERY CAREFUL AND ACCURATE WHEN
USING THEM. KEEP OUT OF REACH OF
CHILDREN.

THE FIRST WATERING AFTER TRANSPLANTING IS THE MOST IMPORTANT ONE. IT SHOULD BE GENTLE BUT THOROUGH ENOUGH TO SETTLE THE SOIL FIRMLY ALL AROUND THE ROOT AREA.

THE PLANT LEAVES MAY REQUIRE 2 TO 6 LIGHT SPRINKLINGS EACH DAY DURING THE FIRST 2 OR 3 DAYS AFTER TRANSPLANTING TO KEEP THE LEAVES FROM SUNBURNING.

PLANTS USUALLY RECOVER FROM TRANSPLANT WILTING IN 2 OR 3 DAYS. THEREAFTER, NORMAL WATERING IS DONE. (SEE CHAPTER 7 FOR NORMAL WATERING.)

WATERING AND FEEDING YOUR PLANTS

7

PLANTS NEED WATER ALL THE TIME. THE AMOUNT VARIES WITH TEMPERATURE, HUMIDITY, WIND, THE TYPE OF SUBSOIL UNDER THE GROW-BOXES, AND WITH THE SIZE AND KIND OF PLANTS. CONDITIONS THAT MAKE YOU THIRSTY AFFECT PLANTS THE SAME WAY.

GIVE THEM WATER WHEN THEY NEED IT! THERE IS NO ARBITRARY "BEST TIME."

PLANT ROOTS DIE (SMOTHER) IN SOIL THAT DON'T DRAIN PROPERLY!

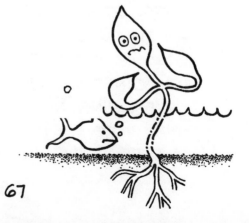

EVERY TIME YOU WATER, PUT ON ENOUGH —
IT'S THE <u>ROOTS</u> THAT NEED IT ! ABOUT
20 MINUTES AFTER WATERING, SOME WATER
SHOULD BE OOZING OUT THE BOTTOM
SIDES OF THE GROW-BOX. ONE OR TWO SUCH
WATERINGS PER WEEK ARE USUALLY
ADEQUATE.

PLANTS CAN BE
WATERED WITH A
SPRINKLING-CAN,
OR A HOSE WITH
SPRAY ATTACHMENT.
YOU CAN USE A HOSE
WITH THE END
CLOTH-COVERED TO
ALLOW FULL
VOLUME WITHOUT
DAMAGING PLANTS
OR ERODING THE SOIL.
THIS GIVES GOOD PENETRATION
AND REDUCES WATERING TIME.

FROM THE END OF THE DEEPEST OR
LONGEST ROOT IN THE SOIL TO THE END OF
THE HIGHEST LEAF-TIP, A PLANT IS A
CONTINUOUS WATER PIPE.

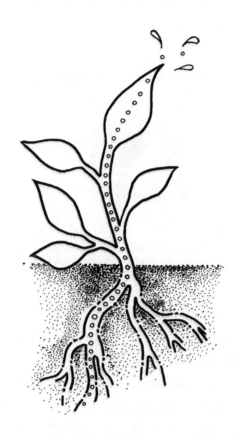

NEARLY 95 PERCENT OF A PLANT'S WEIGHT
IS WATER. <u>EVERY</u> <u>DAY</u> PLANTS LOSE <u>GALLONS</u>
OF WATER (DEPENDING ON PLANT SIZE) TO
THE ATMOSPHERE THROUGH "TRANSPIRATION".

IMPORTANT:
REVISED FEEDING INSTRUCTIONS—
SEE PAGE 74

NOW THAT THE GROW-BOX IS PLANTED, YOU SHOULD BEGIN A REGULAR <u>WEEKLY</u> FEEDING PROGRAM TO SUPPLY PLANTS WITH THE NUTRIENTS NECESSARY TO DEVELOP THE LUSCIOUS VEGETABLE CROPS YOU WANT. (YOUR GROW-BOX ALREADY HAS THE PRE-PLANT FERTILIZER NUTRIENT MIX INCLUDED IN ITS "CUSTOM-MADE SOIL" - CHAPTER 4.)

THE MITTLEIDER METHOD <u>USES DRY, GRANULAR NUTRIENTS</u> FOR THE WEEKLY FEEDING PROGRAM.

THESE ARE PLACED, BY HAND, NEAR THE PLANT. THEY ARE QUICKLY DISSOLVED IN CONTACT WITH WATER IN YOUR REGULAR WATERING PROGRAM. HAND-FEEDING THE PLANTS WITH GRANULAR FERTILIZERS IS VERY EASY AND ACCURATE IF THE NUTRIENTS ARE WEIGHED AND APPLIED CAREFULLY.

HERE IS THE MITTLEIDER NUTRIENT FORMULA FOR YOUR PLANTS WEEKLY FEEDING — THE RESULT OF 30 YEARS EXPERIENCE !

(YOU MAY WRITE THE PUBLISHER FOR UPDATED LIST OF NUTRIENT SUPPLIERS.)

MITTLEIDER NUTRIENT FORMULA
SEE OPTIONAL FORMULA NEXT PAGE.

1. 9 POUNDS CALCIUM NITRATE
2. 4 POUNDS AMMONIUM NITRATE
3. 1½ POUNDS DIAMMONIUM PHOSPHATE
4. 4½ POUNDS POTASSIUM CHLORIDE OR SULFATE
5. 6 POUNDS MAGNESIUM SULFATE (EPSOM SALT)
6. 12 GRAMS BORON (SODIUM BORATE OR BORIC ACID.)
* 7. 8 <u>OUNCES</u> IRON SULFATE
* 8. 4 <u>GRAMS</u> COPPER SULFATE
* 9. 8 <u>GRAMS</u> ZINC SULFATE
* 10. 12 <u>GRAMS</u> MANGANESE SULFATE
* 11. 3 <u>GRAMS</u> MOLYBDENUM (SODIUM MOLYBDATE OR MOLYBDIC ACID.)

* USE ONLY IF NEEDED. USUALLY NOT NEEDED BEFORE 3 OR 4 YEARS OF HEAVY CROP REMOVAL (EXCEPT IN GREENHOUSES).

FEED 1 POUND 4 OUNCES OF THIS DRY NUTRIENT MIXTURE <u>ONCE EVERY WEEK</u> TO EACH STANDARD-SIZE GROW-BOX (5'x30'). <u>STOP</u> FEEDING 2 WEEKS BEFORE HARVESTING THE CROP.

THE FORMULA GIVEN ON PAGE 71 IS
ENOUGH TO FEED <u>ONE</u> STANDARD - SIZE
GROW-BOX (5'x30') FOR 22 WEEKS. IN A
3-TO 5-GALLON CONTAINER WITH TIGHT LID
(PREFERABLY PLASTIC) ACCURATELY WEIGH
THE FERTILIZERS AND MIX <u>ALL</u> TOGETHER
THOROUGHLY. WHEN STORING, KEEP LID
TIGHTLY CLOSED !

FORMULAS FOR GROW-BOXES IN
4-FOOT SECTIONS ARE GIVEN ON
PAGES 180, 181.

OPTIONAL NUTRIENT FORMULA

IF THE COMPLETE NUTRIENT FORMULA ON
PAGE 71 IS UNAVAILABLE, SUBSTITUTE THE
FOLLOWING FORMULA FOR OUTDOOR CROPS,
APPLYING AT THE SAME RATE AS THE REGULAR
FORMULA. (GREENHOUSE CROPS WILL FAIL
IF THE COMPLETE NUTRIENT MIXTURE ON
PAGE 71 IS NOT USED. SEE NOTE PAGE 176.)
WEIGH CAREFULLY AND MIX THOROUGHLY
TOGETHER (DRY):

8 POUNDS AMMONIUM NITRATE

1½ POUNDS DIAMMONIUM PHOSPHATE (21-53-0)

4½ POUNDS POTASSIUM CHLORIDE OR SULFATE

6 POUNDS MAGNESIUM SULFATE (EPSOM SALT)

10 <u>GRAMS</u> BORON (SODIUM BORATE
                    OR BORIC ACID)

NOTE: THE COMPLETE FORMULA ON PAGE 71 AND
THIS SUBSTITUTE FORMULA ARE FOR FEEDING
GROWING PLANTS — NOT TO TAKE THE PLACE OF
THE PRE-PLANT FERTILIZERS (PAGE 48.)

HERE'S HOW YOU APPLY THE DRY FERTILIZER MIX TO THE GROW-BOXES:

WITH THE HAND, JUST BEFORE WATERING, SPREAD A NARROW BAND OF THE FERTILIZER MIXTURE BETWEEN THE PLANT ROWS RIGHT ON THE SOIL SURFACE. IF POSSIBLE, KEEP THE MIXTURE 4 INCHES AWAY FROM STEMS OF PLANTS AND OFF ALL LEAVES.

WATERING DISSOLVES THE FERTILIZERS, THUS THEY MOVE WITH THE SOIL WATER TO THE PLANT ROOTS. FEED PLANTS ONLY ONCE A WEEK NO MATTER HOW MANY TIMES YOU MAY WATER. IF PLANTS SHOW HUNGER SYMPTOMS (SEE APPENDIX III) DO NOT INCREASE THE AMOUNT OF THE FERTILIZER PER APPLICATION. RATHER, FEED TWO TIMES A WEEK FOR TWO WEEKS, THEN RETURN TO THE REGULAR ONCE-A-WEEK FEEDING.   73

GROW — BOX COMMANDMENTS

Follow Explicitly

1. Build the grow-box **level** and substantially strong.

2. Fill the grow-box **level full only** with special soil media.

3. Spread preplant fertilizer formula (page 48) evenly over the entire grow-box surface area.

4. Thoroughly mix the preplant nutrients and grow-box soil together.

5. Water the grow-box heavily before planting seeds or transplanting plants.

6. Plant seeds in rows as shallow as practical (pages 54, 56).

7. Cover seeded area with cheesecloth or burlap until seeds sprout.

8. Water seeded area gently through the cheesecloth and do not move the soil or seeds.

9. Keep the soil surface damp continuously during seed germination.

10. Only use **water** to water unsprouted seeds, — use no fertilizer.

11. Remove cheesecloth immediately after the first tiny sprouts are seen.

Very Important

12. Feed with nutrients (page 71) within 4 to 6 hours after the first tiny sprouts on seeds are seen. Keep nutrients 4 to 6 inches from plants.

13. Feed again two days later same amount of nutrients (page 71).

14. Feed again three days later same amount of nutrients (page 71).

15. All sprouted seeds and transplanted plants require **3 nutrient applications** in the first seven day week period.

16. Feed **once** every **7 days** thereafter until crop matures.

74

HELPING PLANTS GROW

POLLINATION IS USUALLY AUTOMATIC, BUT TRAINING, PRUNING, WEEDING AND PROTECTING PLANTS FROM DISEASE AND PESTS IS NECESSARY. TO MAKE BEST USE OF ALL AVAILABLE SPACE, INCLUDING THE SPACE OVERHEAD, PROVIDE SUPPORT FOR TALLER PLANTS. THIS ALLOWS MORE LIGHT AND AIR, TOO.

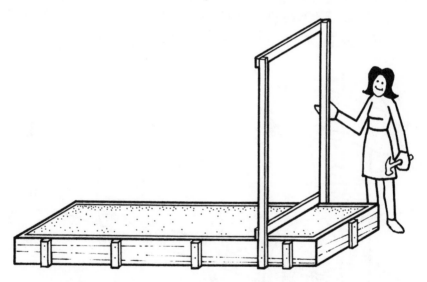

HERE'S HOW TO SUPPORT TALL PLANTS LIKE POLE BEANS, POLE PEAS, TOMATOES, CUCUMBERS, MELONS, AND ZUCCHINI SQUASH. NAIL TO THE OUTSIDE SIDES OF THE GROW-BOX FRAME, 7-FOOT-LONG 1"x 2"s. ACROSS THE TOP OF THE 7-FOOT STAKES AND ACROSS THE TOP EDGE OF THE GROW-BOX SIDES, NAIL 5½-FOOT-LONG 1"x2"s.

75

TIE HEAVY DUTY STRINGS AROUND THE TOP
5½-FOOT 1"x 2" TO CORRESPOND WITH THE PLANTS
IN THE GROW-BOX AND LONG ENOUGH TO TIE
AROUND THE 5½-FOOT 1"x 2" AT THE SOIL LEVEL

WHEN PLANTS GET SO
TALL THEY BEGIN TO FALL
OVER, CAREFULLY GUIDE
THEM AROUND THE STRINGS
IN A CLOCKWISE DIRECTION.
THIS MAY HAVE TO BE DONE
2 OR 3 TIMES A WEEK.

76

TRAINING PLANTS UP
AND AROUND STRINGS
DEMANDS CARE. AVOID
BREAKING, TWISTING,
OR BRUISING THE
STEMS OF
RUNNERS.
TWISTING OR
BRUISING A
STEM KILLS IT.
GENTLY GUIDE THE
RUNNERS AROUND THE

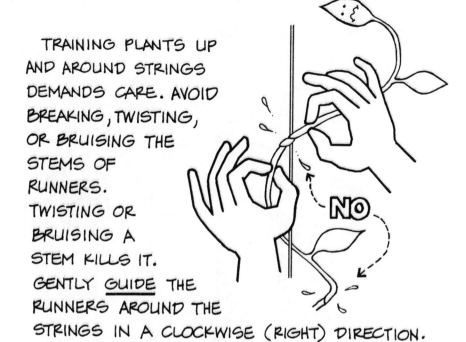

STRINGS IN A CLOCKWISE (RIGHT) DIRECTION.

TOMATOES, CUCUMBERS, MELONS, POLE BEANS
AND POLE PEAS DON'T REQUIRE TYING TO THE
STRINGS AS THEY CLIMB. POLE BEANS WILL
CLIMB THE STRINGS, IF THEY ARE PLACED
PROPERLY, WITHOUT ANY ASSISTANCE.

MORE ZUCCHINI SQUASH
WILL BE PRODUCED
IN A VERY SMALL
AREA IF THE
GROWING END
IS TIED TO A
STRING AS IT
LENGTHENS. THIS
PLANT CANNOT
BE GUIDED
AROUND THE STRING.

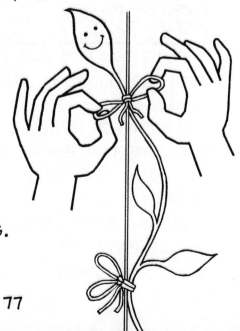

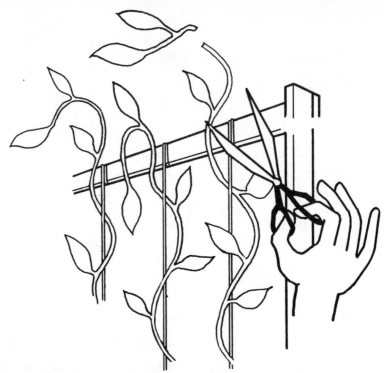

WHEN THE STEMS ARE 8 INCHES HIGHER THAN
THE STRINGS CUT <u>TWO INCHES</u> OFF THE END OF
THE STEM. THIS STOPS THE STEM FROM GROWING
LONGER. PRUNING HELPS A PLANT TO BE MORE
PRODUCTIVE. HERE'S HOW TO PRUNE SEVERAL
KINDS OF PLANTS.

(POLE BEANS AND POLE PEAS)

PLANT 3 SEEDS PER PLANT LOCATION, IN LINE
WITH THE STRINGS. THREE VINES CAN CLIMB A
SINGLE STRING.

WATCH FOR NEW
RUNNERS THAT GROW
OUT FROM THE "AXILS"
OF THE MAIN STEM.
(THE AXIL IS THE UPPER
 ANGLE BETWEEN
 LEAF AND STEM.)

78

CUT THESE NEW RUNNERS OFF **BEHIND** THEIR FIRST LEAF. CUT OFF ONLY THE RUNNERS! **SAVE** THE FLOWER BUDS — THIS IS YOUR FRUIT CROP! THIS IS ALL THE PRUNING REQUIRED, EXCEPT TO REMOVE THE OLDER, YELLOW, DYING LEAVES.

CUCUMBERS AND MELONS ARE PRUNED ALIKE.

PLANT 2 SEEDS PER PLACE. AFTER SEEDS HAVE SPROUTED, PULL OUT THE WEAKER PLANT, LEAVING ONE PLANT PER LOCATION. ALLOW **ONLY ONE** MAIN RUNNER (STEM) TO CLIMB THE STRING. WATCH THE MAINSTEM LEAF NODES (THAT PART OF THE STEM NORMALLY CARRYING A LEAF.). EVERY NODE HAS A BUD. THESE BUDS BECOME NEW RUNNERS. ALLOW THEM TO GROW TO THEIR FIRST LEAF. THERE YOU WILL SEE 3 THINGS.

1. THE LEAF, STEM, AND NODE
2. A SMALL CUCUMBER AND SOME MALE FLOWERS DEVELOPING
3. THE APEX (GROWING TIP OF THE RUNNER)

FOLLOW INSTRUCTIONS CAREFULLY

1. CUT OFF THE YOUNG LEAF. (SHOWN WITH DASHED LINES ON SKETCH).
2. LEAVE THE DEVELOPING CUCUMBER AND MALE FLOWERS IF MALE FLOWERS ARE PRESENT.
3. CUT OFF THE APEX (THE GROWING TIP OF THE RUNNER).

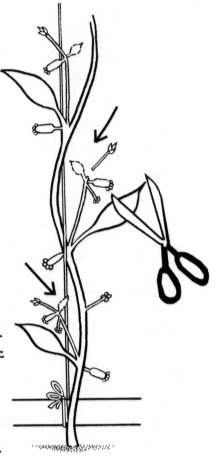

NOTE: AFTER PRUNING, EACH NEW RUNNER WILL HAVE A SMALL CUCUMBER WITH ITS FLOWER BUD AND POSSIBLY SOME DEVELOPING MALE FLOWERS. THE MAINSTEM WILL BE CARRYING LEAVES, CLUSTERS OF MALE FLOWERS, AND CUCUMBERS AT EVERY NODE ALONG ITS ENTIRE LENGTH. DO NOT PRUNE THE MAINSTEM. PRUNE ONLY THE SIDE RUNNERS!

THE NEW RUNNERS, IF NOT PRUNED, WILL
GROW LIKE THE MAIN STEM. THEIR NODES
WILL PRODUCE MORE RUNNERS, ETC; THE
VINES WILL BECOME UNMANAGEABLE, THE
MASS OF FOLIAGE WILL CUT OFF LIGHT
NECESSARY TO DEVELOP FRUIT AND THE
CROP FAILS.
PRUNING PREVENTS
THIS.

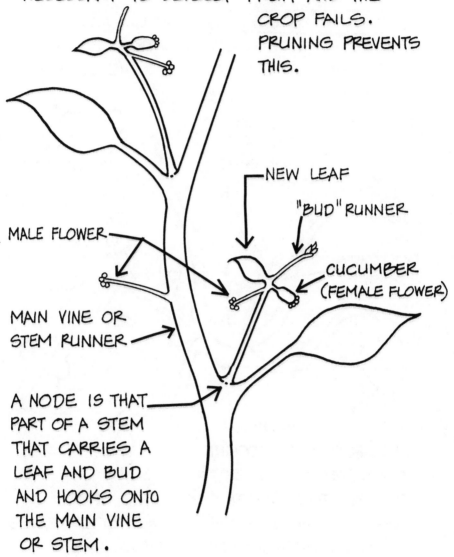

NEW LEAF

"BUD" RUNNER

MALE FLOWER

CUCUMBER
(FEMALE FLOWER)

MAIN VINE OR
STEM RUNNER

A NODE IS THAT
PART OF A STEM
THAT CARRIES A
LEAF AND BUD
AND HOOKS ONTO
THE MAIN VINE
OR STEM.

<u>MELONS OTHER **THAN** WATERMELONS</u> ARE PRUNED THE SAME AS CUCUMBERS.

<u>WATERMELONS</u> REQUIRE SPECIAL PRUNING PROCEDURES. THEY ARE A LAW TO THEMSELVES AND EXPERIENCE IS THE BEST TEACHER.

(ZUCCHINI SQUASH) ARE PLANTED WITH TWO SEEDS AT EACH PLANT LOCATION. BEGIN TYING THE GROWING POINT TO THE STRING WHEN PLANT IS 14 TO 18 INCHES LONG.

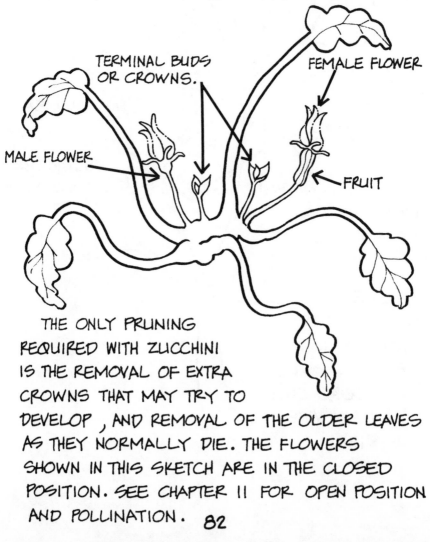

TERMINAL BUDS OR CROWNS.

FEMALE FLOWER

MALE FLOWER

FRUIT

THE ONLY PRUNING REQUIRED WITH ZUCCHINI IS THE REMOVAL OF EXTRA CROWNS THAT MAY TRY TO DEVELOP , AND REMOVAL OF THE OLDER LEAVES AS THEY NORMALLY DIE. THE FLOWERS SHOWN IN THIS SKETCH ARE IN THE CLOSED POSITION. SEE CHAPTER 11 FOR OPEN POSITION AND POLLINATION.

TOMATOES ARE USUALLY GROWN FROM
TRANSPLANTS. SELECT ONLY HEALTHY,
VIGOROUS PLANTS. TIE STRINGS AS YOU
DID FOR CUCUMBERS. AS THE MAINSTEM
GROWS IT WILL PRODUCE NEW SHOOTS
AT EVERY LEAF NODE.

   THESE NEW SIDE SHOOTS MUST BE CUT
OFF OR BROKEN OFF AS SOON AS POSSIBLE.
THE TOMATOES THEMSELVES ARE PRODUCED
ON SEPARATE STEMS OF FLOWERS WHICH
GROW FROM THE MAINSTEM BETWEEN THE
NODES. DO NOT CUT THESE OFF. THESE
FLOWER STEMS PRODUCE THE TOMATOES.

SAVE **ALL** THE TOMATO FLOWERS THAT GROW.
REMOVE **ONLY** THE NEW STEM SHOOTS THAT
GROW OUT AT THE NODES AND THE OLD
YELLOWING LEAVES THAT ARE DRYING.

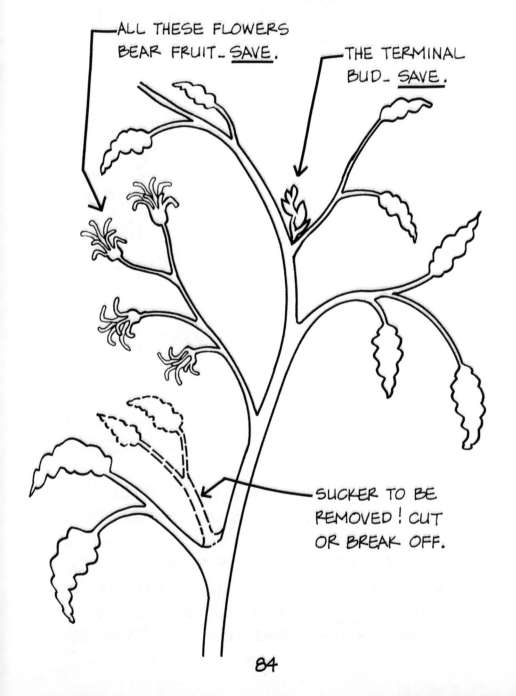

ALL THESE FLOWERS
BEAR FRUIT_ **SAVE.**

THE TERMINAL
BUD_ **SAVE.**

SUCKER TO BE
REMOVED ! CUT
OR BREAK OFF.

PEAS - BUSH REGULAR BUSH PEAS PRODUCE HEAVIER CROPS WHEN THEY ARE GROWN IN GROW-BOXES. PLANT PEAS IN MULTIPLE ROWS. EXAMPLE 2,4,6 ALLOW THE PLANTS TO GROW UPRIGHT UNTIL THEY BEGIN TO FALL OVER.

THEN GENTLY TRAIN THE PLANTS (BY PUSHING OVER) SO THE TWO ROWS LEAN TOWARDS EACH OTHER.

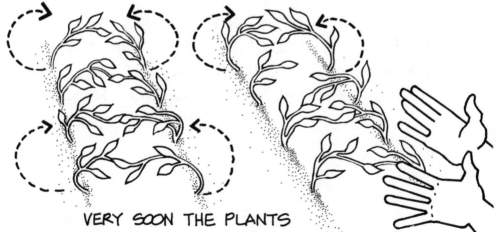

VERY SOON THE PLANTS FASTEN TENDRILS AROUND EACH OTHER AND WILL GROW UPWARD TOGETHER, SUPPORTING EACH OTHER. THUS THE MAIN CROP IS MATURED UP OFF THE GROUND. DOING THIS ELIMINATES STAKING AND TYING AND ACCOMPLISHES THE SAME PURPOSE. 85

WEEDING IS IMPORTANT, BUT WEEDS ARE VERY EASY TO DESTROY AND PULL OUT OF THE SOFT, "CUSTOM-MADE SOIL" IN THE MITTLEIDER GROW-BOXES.

PROTECT YOUR PLANTS FROM DISEASE. THIS STARTS WITH TREATED AND CERTIFIED SEED; BUY PLANTS ONLY FROM REPUTABLE NURSERIES OR GARDEN SHOPS, OR GROW YOUR OWN HEALTHY PLANTS.

KEEP OUT OF YOUR GARDEN ALL DISEASED PLANTS OR OTHER POSSIBLE CONTAMINATED MATERIALS. BURN ALL PLANT PARTS THAT "EVEN" MIGHT BE DISEASED.

THE MITTLEIDER SOIL DRENCH (CHAPTER 6) PREVENTS SOME PROBLEMS RIGHT FROM THE START. CONTINUING PROTECTION, ESPECIALLY FOR INSECT CONTROL, IS BEST "CUSTOMIZED" TO MEET YOUR NEEDS. CONSULT YOUR LOCAL AGRICULTURE AGENCY FOR ADVICE ON SPECIFIC PROBLEMS.

GREENHOUSE SHELTERED GROW·BOXES

SO FAR IN THIS STEP-BY-STEP MITTLEIDER GUIDEBOOK YOU HAVE LEARNED THESE IMPORTANT THINGS:

HOW TO MAKE SIMPLE GARDEN GROW-BOXES.

HOW TO PREPARE "CUSTOM-MADE SOIL".

HOW TO PREPARE A PRACTICAL GARDEN LAYOUT.

HOW TO PLANT YOUR GARDEN GROW-BOX.

HOW TO WATER AND FEED YOUR PLANTS.

HOW TO TRAIN, NURTURE, AND PRUNE YOUR SPECIAL CROPS.

NOW YOU CAN TAKE A GREAT STEP FORWARD BY PROTECTING YOUR GROW-BOX GARDEN WITH A COVERING___YES A GREENHOUSE!

87

BEFORE YOU PANIC....SEE HOW SIMPLE AND EASY IT CAN BE! YOUR GROW-BOX ITSELF CAN SERVE AS THE BASE OF A SIMPLE GREENHOUSE. ONE WAY TO MAKE A SIMPLE SHELTER FOR YOUR GROW-BOX IS TO USE PLASTIC (PVC) PIPE FOR THE FRAME STRUCTURE. THIS PIPE (AT BUILDING SUPPLY STORES) IS LIGHTWEIGHT, STRONG, AND EASY TO USE. IT ALSO PERMITS MAXIMUM LIGHT TO REACH THE PLANTS.

HERE IS A MATERIALS LIST FOR BUILDING A STRONG FRAME TO SUPPORT A PLASTIC COVER.

8-PIECES ¾-INCH PVC PIPE 60-INCHES LONG FOR THE WIDTH.

16-PIECES ¾-INCH PVC PIPE 48-INCHES LONG FOR THE LEGS.

8-PIECES ¾-INCH PVC PIPE 72-INCHES LONG FOR THE CURVED ROOF.

16-PIECES 1-INCH PVC PIPE 15-INCHES LONG FOR HOLDING THE FRAME LEGS.

16-METAL "U" CLAMPS.

50-FEET REGULAR BAILING WIRE.

1-PINT PLASTIC CEMENT.

16-¾-INCH PVC TEES.

16-¾-INCH PVC ELBOWS (45°).

½-POUND 2-INCH-LONG GALVANIZED NAILS.

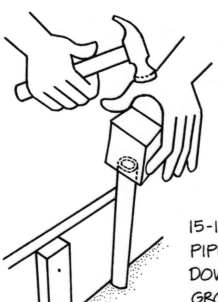

NOTE: THE LENGTHS OF PLASTIC PIPE SHOWN IN THE MATERIALS LIST ARE THE PROPER LENGTHS FOR QUICK ASSEMBLY.

DRIVE THE 1-INCH, 15-INCH-LONG PLASTIC PIPE (LIGHTWEIGHT) DOWN THE SIDES OF THE GROW-BOX (OUTSIDE) UNTIL FLUSH WITH TOP EDGE OF THE SIDE BOARD. START FLUSH WITH THE CORNERS AND SPACE 51½ INCHES APART. THIS WILL GIVE THE CORRECT LOCATIONS ON EACH SIDE OF THE BOX.

TO PREVENT DAMAGE TO THE PLASTIC PIPE USE A WOODEN BLOCK ON TOP OF THE PIPE TO ABSORB THE HAMMER BLOWS.

WITH A METAL "U" CLAMP, NAIL THE 1-INCH PIPE TO THE SIDE BOARD OF THE GROW-BOX.

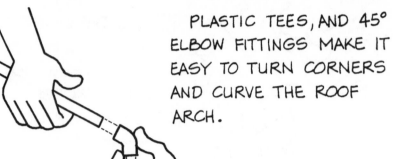

PLASTIC TEES, AND 45°
ELBOW FITTINGS MAKE IT
EASY TO TURN CORNERS
AND CURVE THE ROOF
ARCH.

AFTER CUTTING THE
PLASTIC PIPE INTO
PROPER LENGTHS, GLUE
TOGETHER EACH OF THE
EIGHT FRAMES.
NOTE: THE TOP PIPE
IS CURVED TO PROVIDE THE PITCH OF THE
ROOF. WHEN COVERED WITH PLASTIC IT SHEDS
RAIN QUICKLY.

HERE IS AN EASY WAY TO BE
SURE ALL EIGHT ARCHES ARE
EVEN AT THE RIDGES AND TOP.
MARK EACH PLASTIC LEG THAT
FITS INTO THE 1-INCH PIPE,
6 INCHES FROM END OF
THE PIPE LEG.
DRILL A SMALL
HOLE AT MARK
AND PUSH A 2-INCH
NAIL THROUGH IT.
WHEN THE PIPE IS
SLIPPED INTO THE

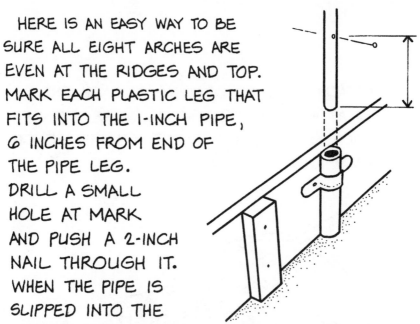

1-INCH PIPE THE NAIL RESTS ON THE TOP
OF THE 1-INCH PIPE AND HOLDS IT AT
THAT POSITION.

AFTER PLACING ALL EIGHT FRAMES,
ATTACH A 1"x2" WOOD SIDE-BOARD WITH
METAL "U" CLAMPS TO THE LEGS OF THE
FRAMES (INSIDE). ALSO ATTACH A 1"x2"
WOOD TIE TO THE RIDGE OF THE CURVED
RIBS (OUTSIDE). USE METAL "U" CLAMPS
TO ATTACH.

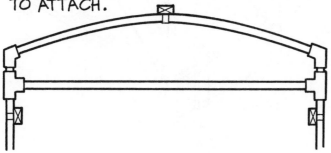

THESE 1"x2" WOOD MEMBERS ALONG THE
TWO SIDES AND AT THE RIDGE WILL
SUPPORT AND TIE ALL THE FRAMES
TOGETHER. 91

ATTACH "X" WIRE BRACING AT EACH END.
ALSO ATTACH ONE DIAGONAL WIRE BRACE
AT EACH SIDE OF THE FIRST FRAME SPACE
AT EACH END.

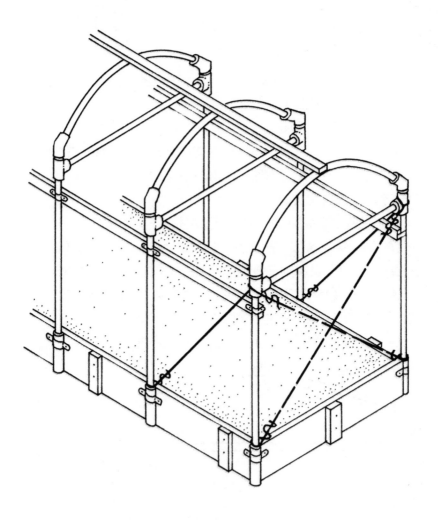

THIS WIRE BRACING STIFFENS
THE STRUCTURE.

WITH ALL THE FRAMES IN PLACE AND PROPERLY BRACED THE STRUCTURE IS READY TO BE COVERED. USE 4-MIL, TRANSPARENT PLASTIC FROM BUILDING SUPPLY COMPANY.

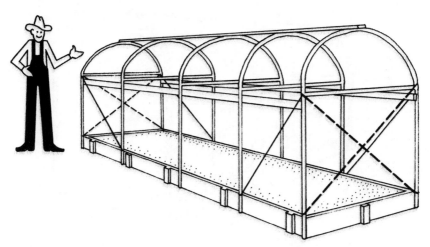

PUT THE END PLASTIC ON FIRST ! STITCH IT WITH NYLON CORD LINE TO THE END FRAMES.
CAUTION : USE STITCHING NYLON CORD THAT RESISTS ROT.

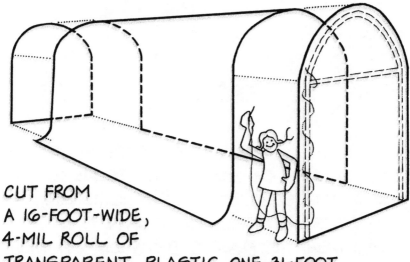

CUT FROM A 16-FOOT-WIDE, 4-MIL ROLL OF TRANSPARENT PLASTIC ONE 31-FOOT LENGTH. THIS WILL COMPLETELY COVER THE STRUCTURE.

LAP THE TOP PIECE OVER THE ENDS AND
STITCH JUST THE CURVED PORTION OF THIS
TOP PIECE TO THE END FRAMES.

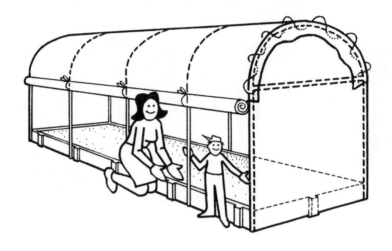

THE SIDES MAY BE ROLLED UP FROM
THE BOTTOM TO PERMIT WORKING THE
GROW-BOXES ; CARING FOR THE CROP, AND
VENTILATION.

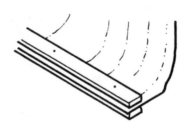

NAIL 1"x 2"x 10'-0" LONG STRIPS OF
WOOD ON EACH SIDE OF THE PLASTIC
NEAR THE EDGE THAT IS ROLLED UP.
NAIL THIS SECURELY-TO TIGHTLY
SANDWICH THE PLASTIC BETWEEN-OR THE
PLASTIC WILL TEAR LOOSE.
(NAIL EVERY 10 INCHES.)

YOU CAN VARY THE GROW-BOX GREENHOUSE
SHELTER. CUT A 10-INCH WALK-WAY DOWN THE
MIDDLE OF THE REGULAR GROW-BOX. PUT A
DOOR IN EACH END AND YOU HAVE ABOUT THE
MOST UNIQUE AND INEXPENSIVE GREENHOUSE
EVER! IN THIS TYPE, THE PLASTIC SIDES ARE
COVERED WITH SOIL AT THE GROUND LEVEL
AND REMAIN FIXED.

THE DOORWAYS PROVIDE VENTILATION.

YOU CAN BUILD YOUR OWN GREENHOUSE
AS SMALL OR COMPLEX AS YOU PREFER.
YOU CAN EVEN BUY A READY-MADE
GREENHOUSE FOR ASSEMBLY IN YOUR
YARD AND MAKE
GROW-BOXES
TO FIT.

THERE ARE MANY GOOD REASONS FOR
GREENHOUSE GARDENING:
CONTROL OF PESTS AND DISEASES.
EXTENDED GROWING SEASON.
CONTINUOUS CROP PRODUCTION.
ENHANCED NUTRITIONAL QUALITY.
CONSERVATION OF WATER AND NUTRIENTS.
PREDICTABLE YIELD AND COSTS.
FAR MORE FOOD ON A GIVEN LAND AREA.
USE LAND OTHERWISE UNSUITABLE
FOR GARDENING.
IN ANY CLIMATE GARDEN CROPS CAN
BE GROWN.

ACTUALLY, THE SUPER-LARGE
FARMING GREENHOUSE IS NOT AS
PRODUCTIVE IN RELATION TO SIZE AS
THE STANDARD-SIZE MITTLEIDER
GREENHOUSE PRESENTED IN THE
NEXT CHAPTER.

MAKING A SIMPLE GREENHOUSE

THE FIRST POINT TO BE DECIDED IS WHERE TO BUILD YOUR GREENHOUSE! PLEASE READ AGAIN CHAPTER 3, "HOW TO MAKE GROW-BOXES". THAT CHAPTER DEALS IN DETAIL WITH LOCATION AND THE SAME INFORMATION APPLIES TO GREENHOUSES. REMEMBER - YOU CAN BUILD OVER ALMOST ANY KIND OF SURFACE IF IT CAN BE LEVELED TO ACCOMMODATE THE GREENHOUSE.

THE STANDARD-SIZE MITTLEIDER GREENHOUSE IS 8 FEET WIDE, 30 FEET LONG, AND 10 FEET HIGH. YOU CAN BUILD ANY SIZE, OF COURSE, TO FIT YOUR PATIO, YARD, OR OPEN AREA! A TYPICAL MITTLEIDER GREENHOUSE REQUIRES NO SPECIAL LABORATORY EQUIPMENT, PUMPS, FANS, PH METERS, TANKS, OR COOLING PADS.

IF SEVERAL GREENHOUSES ARE CONSTRUCTED,
SEPARATE THEM 6 FEET AT THE ENDS AND SIDES.
THIS IS ESSENTIAL FOR ADEQUATE LIGHT
AND AIR.

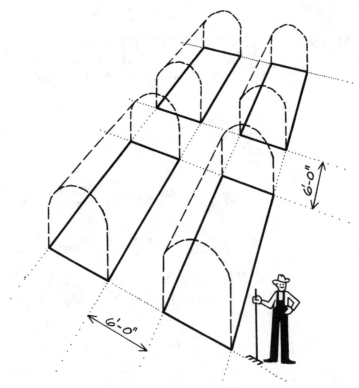

AN AREA 28 FEET BY 42 FEET WILL HOLD
FOUR STANDARD-SIZE GREENHOUSES. MORE
THAN ADEQUATE TO SUPPLY ALL THE FRESH
PRODUCE FOR YOUR FAMILY. A FAMILY CAN
HAVE FRESH PRODUCE AND BE ECONOMICALLY
SELF-SUFFICIENT ON THE INCOME FROM 10
GREENHOUSES. THIS CAN BE ACCOMPLISHED
ON AN AREA OF ONLY 5,000 SQUARE FEET
(1/8 ACRE) ! IF YOU ARE THINKING BIG,
ONE ACRE OF LAND ACCOMMODATES 86
STANDARD-SIZE GREENHOUSES !

HERES HOW TO MAKE THE STANDARD MITTLEIDER GREENHOUSE

LEVEL ENOUGH
GROUND FOR EACH
GREENHOUSE. USE STAKES, CORD, SQUARE, AND
LEVEL TO LINE UP YOUR GREENHOUSE STRAIGHT-
BOTH LENGTH AND WIDTH- AND TO CONSTRUCT IT
PLUMB. STRETCH THE CORD AND TIE IT TO STAKES
THE LENGTH OF ONE SIDE OF THE GREENHOUSE PLOT.

ESTABLISH
AND STAKE THE
FOUR CORNERS
OF THE GREENHOUSE.

MEASURE AND CUT
TO LENGTH, EIGHT
REDWOOD (OR CEDAR)
4"x4" POSTS
9 FEET LONG.
MEASURE AND
MARK 18 INCHES
FROM ONE END
OF EACH OF THE
POSTS. THIS IS THE
PORTION OF THE POST TO BE
EMBEDDED IN THE GROUND.

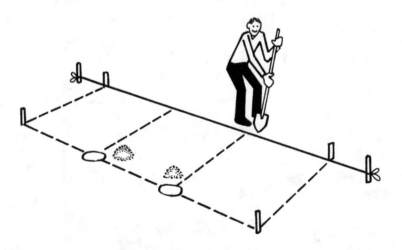

DIG EIGHT HOLES 18 INCHES DEEP WHERE
THE 4"x4" POSTS WILL BE SET.

LOWER A 4"x4" POST INTO CORNER HOLE (a) TO
THE 18-INCH MARK. USE LEVEL TO PLUMB THE
POST (MAKE IT VERTICAL), THEN TAMP IT FIRMLY
INTO PLACE WITH DIRT. THE SECOND POST TO
SET IS THE OPPOSITE CORNER (b); BUT BEFORE
SETTING THIS POST TIGHT, YOU MUST ESTABLISH
THE LEVEL OF THE GREENHOUSE. DO THIS WITH
A CORD, LEVEL, AND CARPENTER'S SQUARE,
LIKE THIS:

DRIVE A NAIL (c) NEAR THE TOP OF POST
(a). TIE THE CORD TO THIS
NAIL.

SQUARE
LEG (d)

LEVEL (e)

SQUARE LEG (f)

(c)

(b)

(a)

PULL THE CORD OVER THE TOPS OF POST (a)
AND THE LOOSE POST (b), APPLYING ENOUGH
TENSION ON THE CORD TO KEEP IT FROM
SAGGING BETWEEN THE POSTS. HOLD THE
SQUARE (d) FLAT AND SQUARE AGAINST
THE LOOSE POST. LINE UP THE OTHER LEG
(f) OF THE SQUARE WITH THE CORD.
PLACE THE LEVEL (e) ON THIS "LEG" OF
THE SQUARE.
IMPORTANT: KEEP THE "LEG" OF THE SQUARE
(f) STRAIGHT WITH THE CORD AT ALL
TIMES (BY MOVING THE TOP OF THE POST
LEFT OR RIGHT). 101

RAISE OR LOWER THE POST (b) UNTIL THE
LEVEL SHOWS "LEVEL" AND THE SQUARE
"LEG" (f) IS <u>PARALLEL</u> WITH AND <u>LEVEL</u>
WITH <u>THE CORD.</u> TAMP THE POST TIGHT
WITH DIRT. IT IS PLUMB, VERTICAL, AND THE
TOP OF THE POST (b) IS LEVEL WITH THE TOP
OF THE POST (a).

NEXT, LOWER POST (g) INTO THE HOLE AT
THE CORNER ON THE OPPOSITE SIDE OF THE
STRUCTURE. THE DISTANCE BETWEEN POSTS
(b) AND (g) IS 8 FEET-INSIDE.
PLACE A STRAIGHT, 2"x4"x10'-0" LONG
BOARD ON TOP OF POSTS (b) AND (g). LAY
THE LEVEL ON TOP OF THE 2"x4". RAISE OR
LOWER POST (g) UNTIL BUBBLE IN LEVEL
READS "LEVEL". NOW, WITH THE LEVEL,
MAKE THE POST (g) VERTICAL AND TAMP
IT FIRM AND SOLID. REPEAT THIS
PROCESS AT THE OTHER END OF THE
STRUCTURE, USING POST (a) TO SET
POST (h) VERTICAL AND LEVEL.

THE FOUR CORNERS ARE ESTABLISHED, LEVEL, AND PLUMB. NOW SET THE SIDE POSTS (TWO ON EACH SIDE).

ON ONE SIDE OF THE STRUCTURE STRETCH A CORD (i) TIGHTLY FROM THE TOP OF ONE CORNER POST OVER THE TOP OF THE OTHER CORNER POST. RAISE OR LOWER THE SIDE POSTS (j) AND (k) UNTIL THEY TOUCH THE STRETCHED CORD OVERHEAD. PLUMB THE POSTS AND TAMP THEM TIGHT.

REPEAT FOR THE OTHER SIDE OF THE STRUCTURE. WITH THIS ACCOMPLISHED THE HARDEST PART OF BUILDING YOUR GREENHOUSE IS DONE. 103

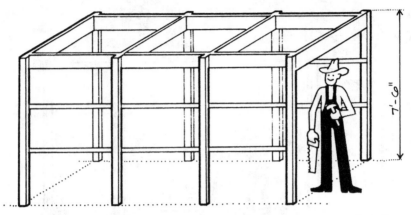

NAIL 2"x 6" BOARDS AROUND THE INSIDE AT
THE TOP OF THE POSTS AND ACROSS THE
WIDTH BETWEEN THE POSTS. NOW JUST
NAIL I"x2" BOARDS SPACED 24 INCHES
APART DOWN THE SIDES ALONG THE LENGTH.

INSTALLING GROW-BOXES

THE BASIC PROCEDURE OF LEVELING AND
INSTALLING THE SIDES OF THE GREENHOUSE
GROW-BOXES IS SIMILAR TO THAT DESCRIBED
IN CHAPTER 3 ON OUTDOOR GROW-BOXES.

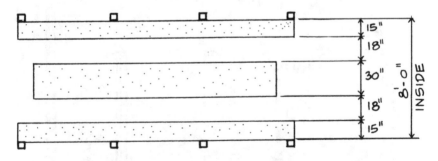

HERE IS A PLAN VIEW OF THE LAYOUT OF
THE GROW-BOXES. THE SIDE BOXES ARE
15 INCHES WIDE, THE AISLES ARE 18 INCHES
WIDE AND THE CENTER GROW-BOX IS
30 INCHES WIDE.

INSTALL 2"x4"
FRAMING AS SHOWN
AT THE ENDS FOR A
DOOR OPENING.
THE DOOR IS
30 INCHES WIDE.
IT IS MADE UP
OF 2"x2" FRAMING
AND HINGED TO
SWING FROM THE
LEFT OUTWARD.

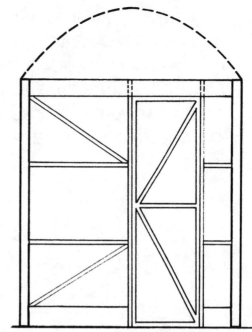

THE DOTTED LINES
SHOW THE SUPPORT
WIRES. THE WIRES RUN THE LENGTH OF THE
GREENHOUSE OVER THE GROW-BOXES.
STRINGS THAT WILL
SUPPORT THE VINES ARE
TIED TO THESE WIRES.

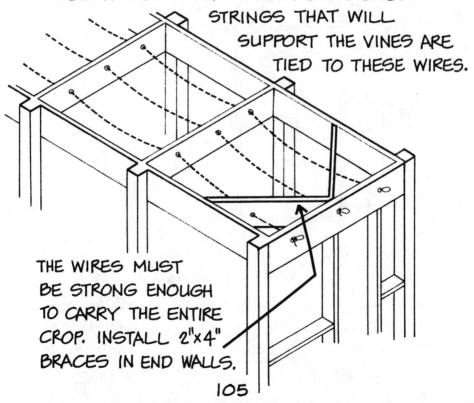

THE WIRES MUST
BE STRONG ENOUGH
TO CARRY THE ENTIRE
CROP. INSTALL 2"x4"
BRACES IN END WALLS.

105

THE WOOD FRAMING AND BRACING IS COMPLETE.
NEXT IS THE PLACEMENT OF THE PLASTIC PIPE
FOR THE CURVED ROOF. THE BASIC PROCEDURE
FOR INSTALLING THIS PLASTIC PIPE IS SIMILAR
TO THAT ALREADY DISCUSSED IN CHAPTER 9
ON GREENHOUSE-SHELTERED GROW-BOXES.

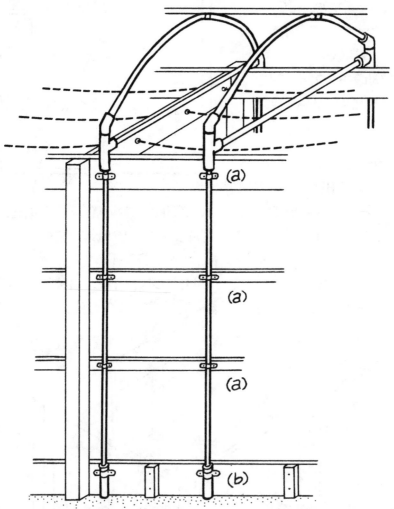

THE PLASTIC PIPE "LEGS" ARE FASTENED TO
THE 1"x 2"'S (a) ALONG THE SIDES AND TO
THE SIDE OF THE GROW-BOX (b); USE METAL
"U" CLAMPS. THE CURVED ROOF MEMBERS ARE
CONNECTED TO THE 2"x2" AT THE RIDGE
WITH "U" CLAMPS ALSO.   106

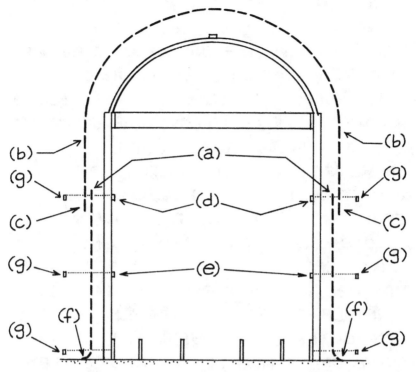

THIS CROSS SECTION INDICATES HOW TO COVER THE STRUCTURE WITH PLASTIC. FIRST, THE 6-FOOT-WIDE SIDE PIECES (a) ARE TACKED IN PLACE JUST ABOVE THE TOP 1"x2" STRIP (d) RUNNING ALONG BOTH <u>SIDES</u> OF THE GREENHOUSE. NEXT, THE 16-FOOT-WIDE PLASTIC TOP-PIECE (b) IS PULLED IN PLACE. THE TOP-PIECE OVERLAPS THE 6-FOOT SIDE-PIECE (c) — ON THE OUTSIDE (TO SHED RAIN). THE TWO PIECES OF PLASTIC (WHEN IN POSITION) ARE FIRST NAILED SECURELY TO THE TOP 1"x2" (d) ON BOTH SIDES OF THE STRUCTURE WITH LATH (g) AND THEN LATHED AND NAILED TO THE LOWER 1"x2" (e) ON BOTH SIDES. THE LOOSE EDGE OF THE PLASTIC ON THE GROUND (f) IS COVERED FIRMLY WITH SOIL THE ENTIRE LENGTH OF THE GREENHOUSE.

THE LATH STRIPS, FASTENING PLASTIC SECURELY TO THE 1"x2"s ON EACH SIDE, AND THE SOIL FIRMLY HOLDING THE PLASTIC TO THE GROUND ANCHOR YOUR PLASTIC COVERING SECURELY AGAINST RAIN AND HARD WINDS.

THERE ARE MANY MODIFICATIONS THAT CAN BE MADE ON THIS BASIC DESIGN. ONE IS REDUCING THE SIZE TO 5 FEET WIDE AND 10, 20, OR 30 FEET LONG-WITH ONLY TWO 15-INCH GROW-BOXES (ONE ON EACH SIDE) AND A 30-INCH AISLE IN THE MIDDLE.

ANOTHER CHANGE IS TO TAPER THE TOP ENDS OF THE 4"x4" POSTS TO MATCH THE CURVE OF THE ROOF. THIS HELPS TO PREVENT THE PLASTIC COVERING FROM TEARING WHEN ONLY ONE LAYER OF PLASTIC IS USED.

NOTE: FOR COLDER WEATHER THE BASIC STANDARD MITTLEIDER GREENHOUSE IS DESIGNED SO THAT IT MAY BE COVERED WITH TWO LAYERS OF PLASTIC WITH A 3-TO 4-INCH, DEAD AIRSPACE BETWEEN THE LAYERS (AN IMPORTANT ECONOMIC FACTOR WHEN HEATING THE GREENHOUSE IS NECESSARY). FOR FURTHER DETAILS ON "COLD WEATHER GARDENING" SEE CHAPTER 12.

SUCCESSFUL GREENHOUSE GARDENING

11

NOW YOU ARE READY TO PREPARE THE GROW-BOXES IN YOUR GREENHOUSE FOR PLANTING. "CUSTOM-MADE SOIL" TO FILL THE THREE GREENHOUSE GROW-BOXES CAN BE THE SAME YOU MADE FOR THE OUTDOOR GROW-BOXES. CHOOSE ANY OF THE COMBINATIONS LISTED IN CHAPTER 4.

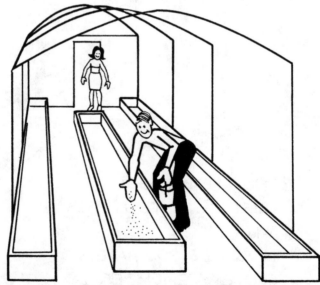

HERE'S HOW TO FILL THE THREE GROW-BOXES IN YOUR GREENHOUSE WITH THE "SOIL MATERIALS".
A) EVENLY SPREAD 2 POUNDS OF GYPSUM OVER THE INSIDE AREA OF EACH 15-INCH BY 30-FOOT GROW-BOX, AND 4 POUNDS GYPSUM OVER THE CENTER 30-INCH BY 26-FOOT GROW-BOX.

NOTE: THE GYPSUM APPLICATION (A) IS TO BE SPREAD ON THE FACE OF THE VIRGIN SOIL AT THE BOTTOM OF THE BOXES BEFORE THE "CUSTOM-MADE SOIL" MEDIA IS ADDED TO FILL THE GROW-BOXES.

B) FILL THE BOXES JUST LEVEL-FULL WITH THE MATERIALS YOU HAVE CHOSEN. REMEMBER DO NOT OVERFILL SO THAT WATER WOULD RUN OFF. DO NOT TAMP OR PACK YOUR "CUSTOM-MADE SOIL".

C) MIX THE MATERIALS THOROUGHLY. A RAKE OR CURVED-TINED RAKE WILL WORK NICELY.

D) WHILE MIXING, ADD JUST ENOUGH WATER
TO PRODUCE A WET MEDIUM, BUT NOT SO
WET THAT YOU COULD SQUEEZE WATER
FROM IT.
NOTE: THE MIXTURE YOU HAVE JUST MADE
CAN BE USED FOR STARTING SEEDS,
TRANSPLANTS, OR FOR GROWING CROPS.

NOW ADD THE PREPLANT FERTILIZER MATERIALS
TO COMPLETE YOUR "CUSTOM-MADE SOIL".

A) CAREFULLY WEIGH AND MIX TOGETHER (DRY)
THE FOLLOWING FERTILIZERS.
    4-POUNDS DOUBLE SUPERPHOSPHATE.
    2-POUNDS POTASSIUM SULFATE
       OR CHLORIDE.
    4-POUNDS SULFATE OF AMMONIA.
    2-POUNDS MAGNESIUM SULFATE
       (EPSOM SALT).
    2-OUNCES (60 GRAMS) BORON
       (SODIUM BORATE OR BORIC ACID).
    12-POUNDS, 2-OUNCES **TOTAL**

B) USE 4 POUNDS OF THIS MIXTURE FOR EACH
15-INCH BY 30-FOOT GROW-BOX. USE
6 POUNDS OF THE MIXTURE FOR THE
30-INCH BY 26-FOOT CENTER BOX.
HERE'S HOW TO DO IT...

C) SPREAD THESE AMOUNTS (B) EVENLY OVER
THE "CUSTOM-MADE SOIL" IN THE
THREE GREENHOUSE GROW-BOXES.

D) NOW, RIGHT ON TOP OF THE FERTILIZER
   MIXTURE, EVENLY SPREAD 1 POUND, 4 OUNCES
   GYPSUM, FOR EACH 15-INCH BOX, AND 2 POUNDS,
   8 OUNCES GYPSUM, FOR EACH 30-INCH
   CENTER BOX.

   NOTE: USE GYPSUM, IF POSSIBLE, FOR LIME
   IN ARID AREAS GETTING LESS THAN 18 INCHES
   RAIN ANNUALLY. IF YOUR AREA GETS MORE
   THAN 20 INCHES OF RAIN PER YEAR, USE
   AGRICULTURAL LIME OR DOLOMITE LIME,
   IF POSSIBLE.

E) MIX EVERYTHING TOGETHER BY HAND OR
   WITH A CURVED-TINED FORK.

F) LEVEL THE MATERIALS IN THE BOXES AND
   ADD BACK ANY "SOIL" THAT SPILLED OUT
   DURING MIXING. BE SURE BOXES ARE
   LEVEL-FULL.

G) SPRINKLE THE SURFACE LIGHTLY TO PREVENT
   RAPID DRYING.

YOUR GREENHOUSE BOXES, THREE PER
GREENHOUSE, ARE READY FOR PLANTING. YOU CAN
PLANT SEED DIRECTLY IN THE BOXES OR YOU CAN
TRANSPLANT SEEDLINGS FROM THE NURSERY OR
FROM YOUR OWN GROWING FLATS.

THE MITTLEIDER GROW-BOX TECHNIQUE YOU
HAVE LEARNED IS THE BASIS FOR SUCCESS IN
GREENHOUSE GARDENING JUST AS IT IS IN
OUTDOOR GROW-BOX GARDENING. ALL THE
BASIC PROCEDURES ARE THE SAME WHETHER
IN THE GREENHOUSE OR OUTDOORS.

HERE ARE SOME DIFFERENCES IN PROCEDURE
BETWEEN GREENHOUSE AND OUTDOOR
GROW-BOX GARDENING.

PLANTS IN THE GREENHOUSE ARE FED A
LARGER AMOUNT OF FERTILIZER. REMEMBER
THAT THE NUTRIENT FORMULAS IN THIS BOOK
ARE CALCULATED FOR THE STANDARD GROWING
AREA SIZE-FOR BOTH THE GROW-BOX AND
THE GREENHOUSE. IF YOU CHANGE THE
DIMENSIONS OF THE BOXES, BE SURE TO
ADJUST THE NUTRIENT AMOUNTS
ACCORDINGLY.

113

HERE AGAIN, IS HOW TO PREPARE YOUR
NUTRIENT MIXTURE. COMBINE DRY
THE FOLLOWING :
   9-POUNDS CALCIUM NITRATE.
   4-POUNDS AMMONIUM NITRATE.
   1½-POUNDS DIAMMONIUM PHOSPHATE
   4½-POUNDS POTASSIUM SULFATE
      OR CHLORIDE.
   6-POUNDS MAGNESIUM SULFATE
      (EPSOM SALT).
   8-OUNCES IRON SULFATE.

   4-GRAMS COPPER SULFATE.
   8-GRAMS ZINC SULFATE.
   12-GRAMS MANGANESE SULFATE.
   12-GRAMS BORON (SODIUM BORATE)
   3-GRAMS MOLYBDENUM (SODIUM
      MOLYBDATE OR MOLYBDIC ACID)

   ALWAYS INCLUDE THESE IN THE GREENHOUSE
FORMULA. USE OUTDOORS IF NEEDED
(SEE APPENDIX II, III).

FROM THE TIME SEEDS ARE SPROUTED OR
PLANTS ARE TRANSPLANTED INTO THE
GREENHOUSE GROW-BOXES THEY ARE FED
6 OUNCES OF THE NUTRIENT MIXTURE
TWO TIMES PER WEEK FOR EACH 15-INCH
BY 30-FOOT GROW-BOX; 12 OUNCES FOR THE
30-INCH BY 26-FOOT CENTER GROW-BOX.

THE FERTILIZER MIX IS SPREAD IN A NARROW
BAND ALONG THE ROWS OF PLANTS (KEEPING
3 TO 4 INCHES AWAY FROM THE PLANT STEMS
THE ENTIRE LENGTH OF THE ROWS). BE CAREFUL
NOT TO GET THE MIX ON THE LEAVES OF THE PLANTS.

AFTER FLOWERING BEGINS (USUALLY 4 TO 6
WEEKS) INCREASE THE FERTILIZER NUTRIENT
AMOUNT TO 12 OUNCES FOR EACH 15-INCH BY
30-FOOT BOX, AND TO
1 POUND, 4 OUNCES FOR
THE 30-INCH BY 26-FOOT
CENTER BOX.

AFTER ABOUT 3 WEEKS OF THE ABOVE
FEEDING INCREASE THE AMOUNTS OF
FERTILIZER NUTRIENTS TO THE FOLLOWING:
1 POUND, 4 OUNCES (MAXIMUM) FOR EACH
15-INCH BY 30-FOOT BOX AND 2 POUNDS,
4 OUNCES (MAXIMUM) FOR THE CENTER
30-INCH BY 26-FOOT BOX.
NOTE: AT THE TIME THE PLANTS ARE
BEING FED THIS LAST INCREASED AMOUNT,
THEY SHOULD BE CARRYING FRUIT,
FLOWERS, AND RAPIDLY INCREASING IN
GROWTH.

IF AT ANY TIME THE PLANTS APPEAR TO BE
NUTRIENT-HUNGRY <u>DO NOT</u> INCREASE THE
FERTILIZER <u>AMOUNTS</u>. INCREASE THE <u>FEEDINGS</u>
FROM 2, TO <u>3</u> PER WEEK FOR ONE OR TWO
WEEKS. THEN RETURN TO THE REGULAR
SCHEDULE.

FOR TRAINING TALL-GROWING AND CLIMBING
PLANTS IN THE GREENHOUSE, TIE ONE END OF
NYLON STRING FOR EACH PLANT TO AN
OVERHEAD WIRE.

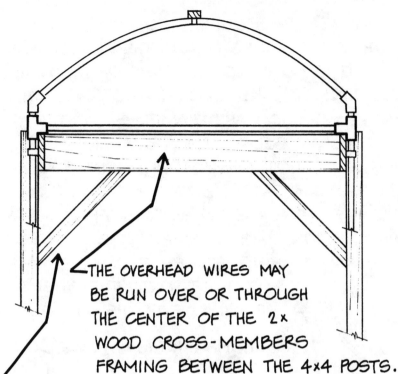

THE OVERHEAD WIRES MAY
BE RUN OVER OR THROUGH
THE CENTER OF THE 2×
WOOD CROSS-MEMBERS
FRAMING BETWEEN THE 4×4 POSTS.
DEPENDING ON THE WEIGHT OF FRUIT TO BE
SUPPORTED BY THE OVERHEAD WIRES, THE 2×
CROSS-MEMBER MAY REQUIRE BRACES TO
THE 4×4 POSTS AS SHOWN.

THE BOTTOM END OF THE STRING FOR TRAINING
TALL-GROWING OR CLIMBING PLANTS IS TIED
TO ANOTHER NYLON STRING AT THE BASE
OF THE PLANTS. THIS ANCHOR
STRING IS ATTACHED TO
EACH END OF THE GROW-BOX.
GENTLY GUIDE THE PLANTS
CLOCKWISE (TO THE RIGHT)
AROUND THE VERTICAL
STRING. DO THIS TWO OR
THREE TIMES A WEEK AS
REQUIRED, AS DISCUSSED
PREVIOUSLY IN CHAPTER 8. PRUNE
IF NECESSARY AT THE SAME TIME.

SOME PLANTS REQUIRE HAND POLLINATION
IN THE GREENHOUSE DURING THE WINTER SEASON
WHEN IT IS KEPT CLOSED MOST OF THE TIME.
ZUCCHINI, MELONS, CUCUMBERS (EXCEPT THE
PARTHENOCARPIC) ARE EXAMPLES. CONTRARY
TO POPULAR BELIEF, TOMATOES AND POLE
BEANS <u>DO NOT</u> REQUIRE ARTIFICIAL POLLINATION
BY SHAKING OR THE BLOWING OF WIND ON THE
PLANTS. HERE ARE SOME POINTERS ON HAND
POLLINATION. THIS IS SIMPLY THE PROCESS
OF TRANSFERRING POLLEN FROM THE MALE
FLOWER ONTO THE STIGMA
(PISTIL) OF THE FEMALE FLOWER.

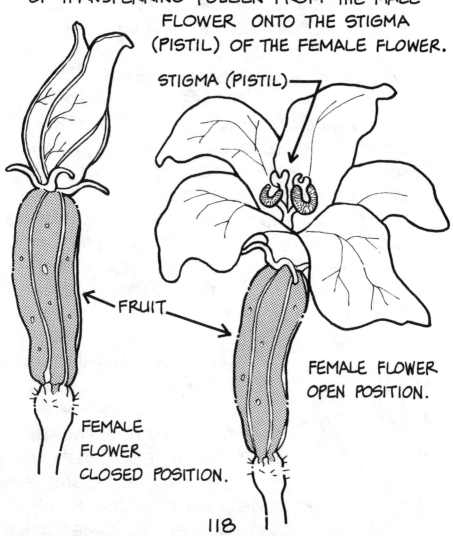

STIGMA (PISTIL)

FRUIT

FEMALE FLOWER
OPEN POSITION.

FEMALE
FLOWER
CLOSED POSITION.

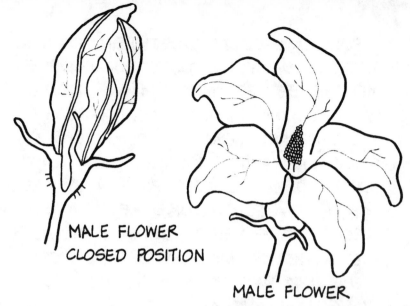

MALE FLOWER
CLOSED POSITION

MALE FLOWER
OPEN POSITION

GENTLY TEAR OFF AND REMOVE THE PETALS
OF THE MALE FLOWER.

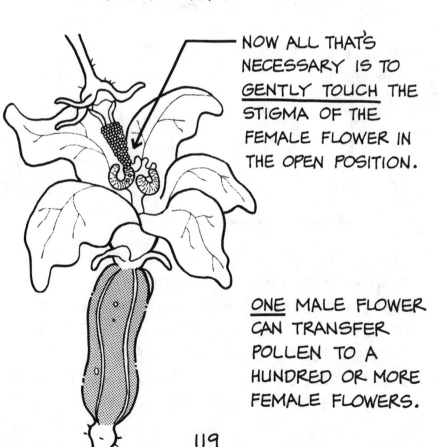

NOW ALL THAT'S
NECESSARY IS TO
GENTLY TOUCH THE
STIGMA OF THE
FEMALE FLOWER IN
THE OPEN POSITION.

ONE MALE FLOWER
CAN TRANSFER
POLLEN TO A
HUNDRED OR MORE
FEMALE FLOWERS.

119

POLLINATE SQUASH BETWEEN 7:00 AND
9:00 A.M. DAILY. POLLINATE CUCUMBERS, AND
MELONS BETWEEN 11:00 A.M. AND 2:30 P.M.
DAILY. POLLINATE ONLY HEALTHY, FRESH,
FULLY OPENED FEMALE FLOWERS. POLLINATE
DAILY FOR MAXIMUM FRUIT SET (CONTINUE
FOR 12 TO 15 WEEKS). POLLEN IS VIABLE
FOR JUST A FEW HOURS AS IS ALSO THE
RECEPTIVE STAGE OF FEMALE FLOWERS.

EVEN THOUGH MOST VEGETABLE CROPS DO
WELL IN A RATHER WIDE TEMPERATURE
RANGE THEY USUALLY DO BEST BETWEEN
75°F AND 85°F. THE OBJECTIVE IN EITHER
HEATING AND VENTILATING YOUR GREENHOUSE
IS TO MAINTAIN THIS IDEAL RANGE.

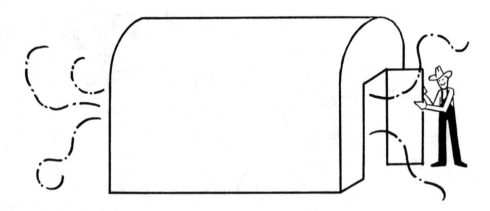

EASE OF VENTILATION IS ONE OF THE BEST
FEATURES OF SMALL GREENHOUSE
GARDENING. THE DOORS ON EACH END OF
THE GREENHOUSE ARE ADEQUATE TO GIVE
PROPER VENTILATION UP TO 80°F. THE
DOORS CAN BE OPENED 6 INCHES OR WIDE
OPEN TO PROVIDE THE AIR NEEDED.

AT HIGHER TEMPERATURES, ADDITIONAL COOLING CAN BE PROVIDED BY OPENING THE PLASTIC ARCHES BETWEEN THE TOP OF THE DOOR FRAMES AND THE TOP OF THE GREENHOUSE. ANOTHER METHOD IS TO WHITEWASH THE TOP OF THE GREENHOUSE. IN PLACES WHERE TEMPERATURES COMMONLY REACH 95°F TO 115°F YOU CAN USE SARAN NETTING, 46 TO 52 PERCENT SHADE, TO COVER YOUR GREENHOUSE. IN THIS CASE THE ENDS ARE NOT COVERED.

HERE ARE SOME TIPS FOR REGULATING TEMPERATURES AND VENTILATION:

IN LATE SPRING AND SUMMER, OPEN THE DOORS BY 7:00 A.M. FOR VENTILATION. CLOSE THEM BY 6:00 P.M. TO KEEP OUT THE NIGHT-FLYING MILLERS.

ON DAYS WITH TEMPERATURES BELOW 55°F KEEP THE DOORS CLOSED. AT THIS TEMPERATURE PLANTS ARE NEARLY DORMANT AND TRANSPIRATION IS VERY LOW.

WATERING IN THE GREENHOUSE IS USUALLY DONE TWICE WEEKLY. FOR LARGE PLANTS IN THE HEAT OF SUMMER INCREASE TO 3 WATERINGS WEEKLY. DURING THE WINTER SEASON WHEN PLANTS ARE NEARLY DORMANT, WATER ONCE A WEEK - OTHERWISE THE AMOUNTS OF WATER APPLIED AND APPLICATION TECHNIQUES ARE THE SAME AS WITH THE OUTDOOR GROW-BOXES (CHAPTER 7).

COLDWEATHER GARDENING

12

YOU CAN ENJOY THE
PLEASURES OF
GARDENING EVEN IN
THE COLDEST WEATHER
IF YOU PROVIDE
ADEQUATE SHELTER
AND WARMTH.
AT 50°F OR LOWER,
PLANTS BECOME DORMANT. AT 32°F MANY
WILL DIE. GREENHOUSE GARDENING
REDUCES THE NUMBER OF "NO-GROWTH"
DAYS. IN SEVERE WEATHER, OF COURSE,
GREENHOUSE HEATING DOES COST MONEY.
THIS CHAPTER SHOWS YOU SEVERAL WAYS
TO MINIMIZE SUCH COSTS.

HERE ARE RECOMMENDATIONS FOR
GREENHOUSE GARDENING IN THREE
DIFFERENT CLIMATIC AREAS - MILD,
MODERATE, AND COLD.

MILD CLIMATE

GREENHOUSE GARDENS ARE EASY TO
MANAGE IN MILD AREAS. DOUBLE-WALL
(2-OR 4-MIL TRANSPARENT PLASTIC)
TIGHTLY BUILT, PLASTIC GREENHOUSES

ARE ADEQUATE TO KEEP PLANTS GROWING STEADILY ALL WINTER WITHOUT ARTIFICIAL HEAT OF ANY KIND. DAYTIME TEMPERATURES FROM 45°F TO 75°F AND NIGHTTIME TEMPERATURES NEVER LOWER THAN 27°F ARE CONSIDERED TO BE MILD CLIMATE CONDITIONS. JUST CLOSE THE DOORS OR VENTILATION DEVICES EARLY IN THE AFTERNOON TO CONSERVE AND BUILD UP SOIL HEAT TO CARRY THROUGH THE NIGHT.

MODERATE CLIMATE

DAYTIME TEMPERATURES BETWEEN 40°F AND 60°F AND NIGHTTIME TEMPERATURES DOWN TO 13°F ARE CONSIDERED TO BE MODERATE CLIMATE CONDITIONS. THE COLD SEASON IN SUCH A CLIMATE IS ABOUT 12 WEEKS. IF ENOUGH HEAT IS SUPPLIED, OF COURSE, PLANTS CAN BE GROWN NORMALLY IN THE GREENHOUSE ALL WINTER, BUT COSTS MAKE GROWING DURING THE COLDEST WEEKS ECONOMICALLY UNSOUND.

JUST PLANT THE CROP TO TAKE ADVANTAGE OF NATURE'S FREE SUMMER HEAT, SO THAT PLANTS REACH MAXIMUM FRUIT SET AND VEGETATIVE GROWTH BY AUTUMN. THEN ALLOW THE PLANTS TO GROW AT THE MUCH REDUCED RATE CAUSED BY LOWER TEMPERATURE. THEY WILL GRADUALLY MATURE DURING DECEMBER AND JANUARY.

HERE IS AN EXAMPLE

1) TOMATOES CAN BE <u>SEEDED</u> BY JULY 1, TRANSPLANTED INTO FLATS OR 4-INCH POTS AND GROWN UNTIL AUGUST.

2) PREFERABLY BEFORE AUGUST 15 THESE PLANTS SHOULD BE TRANSPLANTED INTO THE GREENHOUSE. THEY WILL REACH THEIR MAXIMUM GROWTH AND FRUIT SET BETWEEN NOVEMBER AND DECEMBER 1.

YOU NEED ONLY ENOUGH ARTIFICIAL HEAT TO KEEP THE TEMPERATURE JUST ABOVE 32°F.

3) NOT LATER THAN OCTOBER 10, THE SECOND
LAYER OF PLASTIC SHOULD BE STRETCHED
OVER THE GREENHOUSE.
THIS SECOND
LAYER WILL
PRODUCE A
DEAD-AIR
SPACE.
WITH THE USE OF
PLASTIC PIPE
ANOTHER FRAME
FOR THE
TRANSPARENT
PLASTIC COVERING
IS BUILT <u>OVER</u>
THE FIRST FRAME
AND COVERING.
SEE MATERIALS
LIST FOR THIS
FRAME IN
APPENDIX IV.

126

HERE IS A CLOSER LOOK AT THE RELATIONSHIP
OF THE FRAMEWORK OF THE DOUBLE-WALL
CONSTRUCTION TO ACHIEVE THE DEAD-AIR
INSULATION SPACE. FOR THE SAKE OF CLARITY
THE PLASTIC COVERING ON THE FIRST STRUCTURE
IS NOT SHOWN.

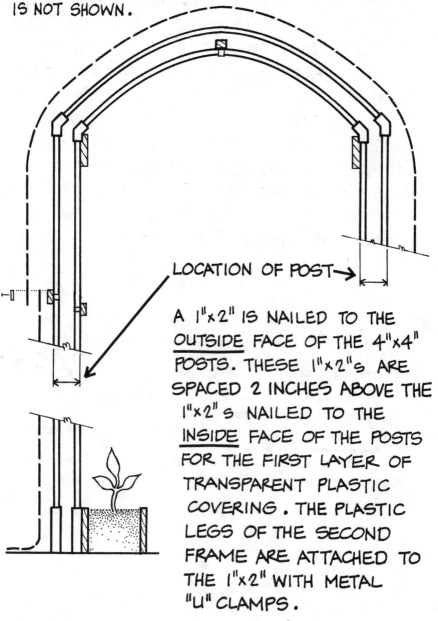

LOCATION OF POST→

A 1"x2" IS NAILED TO THE
OUTSIDE FACE OF THE 4"x4"
POSTS. THESE 1"x2"s ARE
SPACED 2 INCHES ABOVE THE
1"x2"s NAILED TO THE
INSIDE FACE OF THE POSTS
FOR THE FIRST LAYER OF
TRANSPARENT PLASTIC
COVERING. THE PLASTIC
LEGS OF THE SECOND
FRAME ARE ATTACHED TO
THE 1"x2" WITH METAL
"U" CLAMPS.

AT THE GROUND LEVEL THE FRAME LEGS ARE INSERTED IN THE THIN WALL PLASTIC PIPE 4-INCHES AWAY FROM THE FIRST FRAME. THE TRANSPARENT PLASTIC (6-FEET-WIDE STRIPS) IS PUT ON THE SIDES FIRST. THE TOP PIECE OF PLASTIC IS THEN PUT ON AND LAPPED OVER AT THE SPLICE LOCATION. A WOOD LATH IS THEN NAILED OVER THIS HORIZONTAL SPLICE TO THE 1"x2".

ON THE ENDS OF THE GREENHOUSE ONE LAYER OF PLASTIC IS LATHED ON THE INSIDE AND ANOTHER LATHED ON THE OUTSIDE OF THE 2"x4" FRAMEWORK-DOORS INCLUDED-THUS, PROVIDING A DEAD-AIR SPACE.

MITTLEIDER GREENHOUSES ARE EASY TO MAKE AND VERY EFFECTIVE.

SINGLE TRANSPARENT
PLASTIC WALL .

TWO TRANSPARENT PLASTIC WALLS
WITH DEAD-AIR SPACE .

4) ALSO FOR MODERATE CLIMATE REGIONS, PROVIDE ACCEPTED INSTALLATIONS FOR ARTIFICIAL HEAT BEFORE OCTOBER 10. ELECTRIC HEAT LAMPS, TOTALING 900 TO 1200 WATTS WILL WORK. THIS ARTIFICIAL HEAT WILL BE USED THROUGH FEBRUARY 15 ONLY AS NEEDED TO KEEP THE TEMPERATURE JUST ABOVE 32°F. THE COST SHOULD BE MODERATE.

5) ON FEBRUARY 15, THE OLD TOMATO VINES ARE REMOVED AND NEW PLANTS TRANSPLANTED BY FEBRUARY 20. THIS SECOND CROP CAN BE HARVESTED DURING MAY, JUNE AND JULY. THIS SCHEDULE ALLOWS HARVESTING <u>TWO</u> OUT-OF-SEASON CROPS <u>YEARLY</u> WITH MINIMAL HEATING EXPENSE.

<u>COLD CLIMATE</u>

GREENHOUSE CROPS CAN BE GROWN IN AREAS HAVING VERY COLD WINTER TEMPERATURES OF PLUS 10°F TO MINUS 30°F FOR ONE-OR TWO-WEEK CYCLES;

AND AVERAGE. DAYLIGHT TEMPERATURES
BETWEEN 20°F AND 45°F. PLANNING FOR WINTER
CROPS IN SUCH AREAS SHOULD BEGIN WITH
GREENHOUSE LOCATION AND CONSTRUCTION.

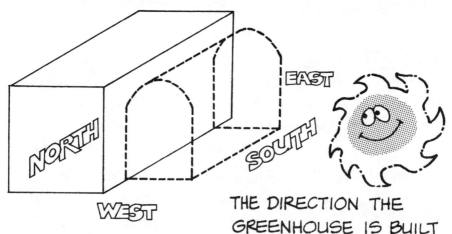

THE DIRECTION THE
GREENHOUSE IS BUILT
IS IMPORTANT. HEATING COSTS CAN BE REDUCED
BY PLACING THE GREENHOUSE EAST AND WEST.
THE NORTH-SIDE WALL CAN EVEN BE DUG
INTO THE SOUTH SLOPE OF A HILL, OR
PLACED AGAINST A
WALL LEAVING THE
SOUTH SIDE EXPOSED
TO THE SUN.

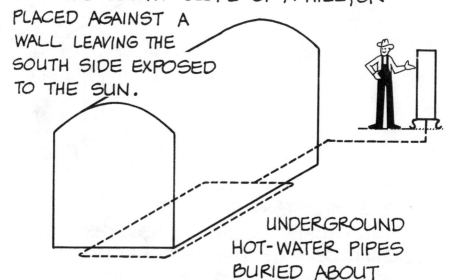

UNDERGROUND
HOT-WATER PIPES
BURIED ABOUT
6 INCHES DEEP INSIDE THE GREENHOUSE
(ALONG THE OUTER EDGES) WILL WARD
OFF COLD FROM THE FROZEN GROUND
OUTSIDE.

WITH ONLY THESE PRECAUTIONS, A PLANTING
SCHEDULE LIKE THE EXAMPLE DESCRIBED IN
MODERATE CLIMATE SHOULD PRODUCE VERY
SATISFACTORY RESULTS.

VENTILATION

IN AUTUMN, WINTER, AND EARLY SPRING-
IN ANY CLIMATE- EACH DAY'S TEMPERATURE
WILL DETERMINE HOW MUCH, IF AT ALL,
TO OPEN THE DOORS. AS A RULE, WHEN DAY
TEMPERATURE REACH 65°F OPEN THE
DOORS ABOUT 6 INCHES,
EVEN IF IT IS ONLY FOR
AN HOUR OR TWO IN THE
MIDDLE OF THE
DAY.

THE IMPORTANT THING IS
TO VENTILATE AS MUCH AS POSSIBLE
BUT CLOSE UP THE GREENHOUSE
EARLY ENOUGH TO KEEP THE SOIL
TEMPERATURES WELL ABOVE 50°F AS
LONG AS POSSIBLE FOR MAXIMUM
GROWTH.

<u>WHAT WE HAVE SEEN IN THIS CHAPTER</u> IS THAT NORMAL GROWING OF CROPS IN THE WINTER MONTHS MAY NOT BE ECONOMICAL IN ALL AREAS. BUT YOU CAN GROW A CROP TO NEAR MATURITY IN DECEMBER AND LET IT MORE OR LESS <u>COAST</u> THROUGH DECEMBER AND JANUARY BY JUST KEEPING IT ALIVE. THE FRUIT <u>WILL</u> STILL RIPEN DESPITE THE WINTER COLD AND YOU CAN TAKE ADVANTAGE OF HIGH OUT-OF-SEASON PRICES WITHOUT EXCESSIVE HEATING COSTS.

Producing your own seedlings for transplanting is pleasant work — and a real economy, especially if you are planting a number of grow-boxes.

STARTING SEEDLINGS FOR TRANSPLANTING

13

STARTING YOUR GARDEN
FROM TRANSPLANTS RATHER
THAN SEEDS WILL PRODUCE GREATER YIELDS
AND 8 TO 12 WEEKS EARLIER. THIS IS MORE
TRUE OF SMALL SEED PLANTS LIKE TOMATO
AND PEPPER THAN FOR BEANS OR SQUASH.
TRANSPLANTS COST QUITE A BIT, UNLESS
YOU GROW THEM YOURSELF. THIS CHAPTER
TELLS YOU HOW TO DO IT.

MAKE 3 OR 4 BOXES (FLATS)
18 INCHES SQUARE BY
3 INCHES DEEP. THE
BOTTOMS CAN BE MADE
WITH SLATS, AT LEAST
THREE, SEPARATED
1/8-INCH FOR DRAINAGE.

135

FILL THESE FLATS WITH THE "CUSTOM-MADE SOIL"
USED IN YOUR GROW-BOXES OR GREENHOUSE,
WITHOUT THE PRE-PLANT FERTILIZER. SPREAD
OVER EACH FILLED FLAT ½-OUNCE LIME, AND
½-OUNCE DOUBLE SUPERPHOSPHATE (ABOUT
2 TABLESPOONS OF EACH).
ADD WATER AND MIX
THOROUGHLY SO THAT
THE SOIL IS QUITE
WET BUT NOT SO
WET THAT YOU CAN
SQUEEZE WATER
FROM IT.

LEVEL THE SOIL
SURFACE AND MARK
FOR 8 ROWS
PER FLAT.

SEEDS MAY BE SOWN QUITE
CLOSE TOGETHER (ABOUT
600-1000 SEEDS
PER EACH FLAT).
BEWARE OF PLANTING
SO MANY SEEDS
THAT PLANTS WILL
BE CROWDED. THIS
PRODUCES SMALL,
WEAK SEEDLINGS.

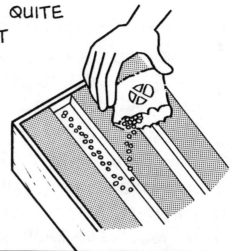

HERE IS GOOD SPACING IN THE SEED
BOXES (FLATS) FOR A FEW KINDS
OF SEED.

┌─SEEDS PER ROW─┐

CABBAGE	100-125	CAULIFLOWER	100-125
LETTUCE	100-125	BROCCOLI	100-125
TOMATO	100-125	CELERY	200-250
PEPPERS	100-125	PARSLEY	200-250
BEETS	50-75	SWISS CHARD	50-75

COVER THE SEEDS LIGHTLY, ABOUT 2½-TIMES
THEIR THICKNESS, WITH THE "CUSTOM-MADE SOIL"
(CHAPTERS 2 AND 11). SPRINKLE THE SOIL
MODERATELY. COVER WITH A PIECE OF BURLAP
AND KEEP IT MOIST UNTIL YOU SEE THE
FIRST SPROUTS. THEN, PLACE THE FLATS
WHERE THE NEW PLANTS WILL RECEIVE AS
MUCH LIGHT AS POSSIBLE. IF WEATHER
IS COLD, KEEP THESE FLATS IN A
GREENHOUSE OR A SHELTERED PORCH.

AFTER SEEDS HAVE SPROUTED, WATER
JUST ENOUGH TO PROVIDE FOR
SATISFACTORY GROWTH.

IMPORTANT :

EVERY WATERING AFTER SEEDS HAVE
SPROUTED IS WITH THE FOLLOWING
WATER-FERTILIZER SOLUTION. IN 55 GALLONS
OF WATER (GASOLINE DRUM) DISSOLVE :
    8-OUNCES OF AMMONIUM NITRATE.
    2-OUNCES OF MAGNESIUM SULFATE.
    2-OUNCES OF POTASSIUM SULFATE
       OR CHLORIDE.
    2-OUNCES OF DIAMMONIUM PHOSPHATE
    REMEMBER THIS SOLUTION IS THE ONLY
LIQUID YOU USE TO WATER THE
SEEDLINGS, AFTER THEY HAVE SPROUTED,
FOR 4-TO 6-WEEKS.

SEEDLINGS ARE READY FOR TRANSPLANTING
WHEN THEY HAVE GROWN THEIR FIRST OR
SECOND SET OF TRUE LEAVES (ABOUT
TWO OR THREE INCHES HIGH). SEEDLINGS
ARE USUALLY TRANSPLANTED TO
ANOTHER FLAT, 81 TO A FLAT, OR INTO
3-AND 4-INCH POTS-USING THE
"CUSTOM-MADE SOIL".

HERE IS AN EXAMPLE OF A SIMPLE MARKER
MADE WITH 81 ½-INCH-DIAMETER DOWELS.
THIS WILL SAVE YOU TIME IN PREPARING
YOUR FLATS FOR PLANTING.

THEY ARE KEPT IN A WARM SEEDHOUSE
OR GREENHOUSE AND ENCOURAGED
(WITH ENOUGH HEAT) TO GROW FOR 4 TO 8
WEEKS (DEPENDING ON THE VARIETY).
WHEN WEATHER PERMITS, THEY ARE
PLANTED OUTDOORS OR INTO THE
GREENHOUSE WHERE THEY WILL FRUIT
AND MATURE.

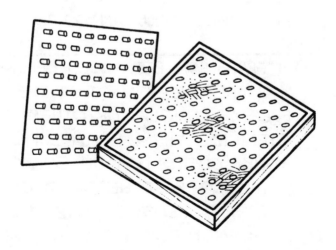

YOU CAN FOLLOW THESE SAME PROCEDURES
FOR JUST A FEW SEEDLINGS IN THE SMALL
FLATS AS DESCRIBED, OR USE A REGULAR,
LARGE GROW-BOX (5'x30') TO START MANY,
YES THOUSANDS, OF SEEDLINGS TO PLANT
A LARGE CROP.

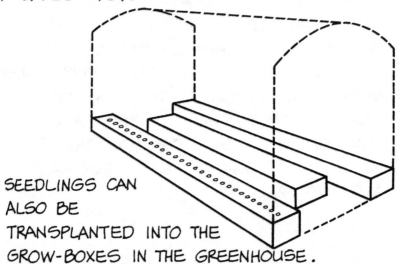

SEEDLINGS CAN
ALSO BE
TRANSPLANTED INTO THE
GROW-BOXES IN THE GREENHOUSE.

YOUNG SEEDLINGS ARE VULNERABLE TO
FUNGUS DISEASES AND PESTS. HERE ARE
SOME THINGS YOU CAN DO TO PROTECT
THEM.

1) IF FLATS HAVE BEEN USED BEFORE AND
   YOU ARE UNCERTAIN THAT THEY ARE
   FREE OF FUNGUS OR OTHER DISEASES,
   STERILIZE THEM BEFORE FILLING WITH
   YOUR "CUSTOM-MADE SOIL".

   THIS CAN BE DONE BY STACKING THEM
   UNDER A PLASTIC COVERING AND
   FUMIGATING WITH STEAM OR
   METHYL BROMIDE (FROM YOUR FARM
   AND GARDEN SUPPLY SHOP).

BE CAREFUL IN USING METHYL BROMIDE.
FOLLOW INSTRUCTIONS ON THE LABEL
CAREFULLY. SEAL THE PLASTIC TO THE GROUND
WITH DIRT SO FUMES DON'T ESCAPE. LEAVE
24 TO 48 HOURS, THEN EXPOSE TO THE AIR
SEVERAL HOURS BEFORE USING.

2) YOU CAN STERILIZE THE FLATS ONE AT A
TIME JUST BY PLACING THEM IN AN OVEN
(250°F) FOR 45 MINUTES. ANOTHER
METHOD IS TO COVER THE FLATS WITH
BOILING WATER; ALWAYS BE CAREFUL.

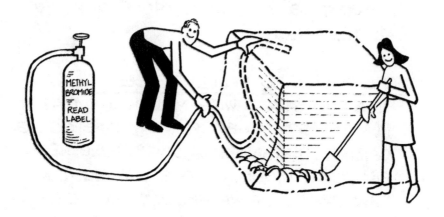

YOU CAN STERILIZE TRAYS (FLATS) AND THE
SOIL AT THE SAME TIME BY FILLING THE TRAYS
AND STACKING THEM. STACK THEM WITH
ROOM FOR AIR CIRCULATION BETWEEN. THEN
USE THE METHYL-BROMIDE TREATMENT AS
PREVIOUSLY DESCRIBED. THIS METHOD IS
ESSENTIAL IF YOU ARE STARTING
SEEDLINGS IN FLATS OR IN A REGULAR
GROW-BOX FOR LARGE SCALE PRODUCTION.

USE CERTIFIED SEED, IF POSSIBLE, TO
MINIMIZE DISEASE PROBLEMS. HERE IS HOW TO
TREAT YOUR OWN SEED, IF YOU WISH.

    a) GIVE SOME SMALL SEEDS (LIKE CELERY
       AND TOMATO) A HOT WATER BATH
       (130°F) FOR 30 MINUTES.

    b) YOU CAN ALSO "PELLETIZE" SEED.
       THIS CONSISTS OF COATING THE SEEDS
       WITH A FUNGICIDE POWDER. SOME
       FUNGI ARE CARRIED INSIDE THE SEED.
       IT BECOMES ACTIVE ONLY WHEN THE
       SEED GERMINATES. A FUNGICIDE
       COATING WILL KILL THEM RIGHT AT
       THE START.

HERE IS HOW TO PELLETIZE SEED:

1) IN A ONE-QUART, WIDE-MOUTH JAR OR
   PLASTIC CONTAINER PUT 1/8-TEASPOON OF
   CAPTAN, DIATHANE OR OTHER FUNGICIDAL
   PRODUCT. DISSOLVE THIS WITH JUST A
   FEW DROPS OF WATER. PUT THE SEEDS IN
   THE CONTAINER AND ROLL THEM AROUND
   WITH YOUR FINGERS TO GET AN EVEN
   WETTING AND COATING ON THEM. THIS
   AMOUNT OF MATERIAL WILL COAT AT
   LEAST 500 OF ANY KIND OF SEEDS.

2) NEXT ADD JUST ENOUGH
   AGRICULTURAL LIME (NOT BURNED LIME)
   TO ABSORB THE MOISTURE. ROLL THE
   SEEDS AND LIME TOGETHER.

3) SEEDS CAN BE SOWN IMMEDIATELY
   OR STORED FOR FUTURE USE.
4) KEEP SEED FLATS OR BEDS
   IN SHELTERED AREA OR IN
   A GREENHOUSE WITH
   SCREENED OPENINGS
   TO KEEP INSECTS
   OUT.
5) IF NECESSARY,
   USE PREVENTIVE
   SPRAY PROGRAMS
   APPRORIATE TO
   YOUR REGION'S
   PROBLEMS. YOUR
   LOCAL AGRICULTURAL
   OFFICERS CAN HELP
   YOU A LOT.

6) IN TRANSPLANTING YOUNG SEEDLINGS,
   FOLLOW THE PROTECTIVE PROCEDURES
   IN CHAPTER 6 AND 11.
7) BE SANITATION CONSCIOUS! CAREFULLY
   INSPECT ALL PLANTS OR SEEDS BEFORE
   TAKING THEM INTO YOUR GARDEN. IF
   THEY SHOW SIGNS OF DISEASE, BURN
   THEM, EVEN IF THEY CAME FROM
   WELL-MEANING FRIENDS.

> I DO NOT HESITATE TO RECOMMEND THE
> NECESSARY USE OF INSECTICIDES. IT IS
> OFTEN A SIMPLE QUESTION OF USING THEM
> OR LOSING YOUR CROP! YOU OFTEN HAVE
> TO MAKE THAT CHOICE.

THE MITTLEIDER METHOD IN OPEN FURROW

14

YOU CAN USE MITTLEIDER GARDENING METHODS RIGHT IN THE COMMON SOIL, IF YOU WISH. IT IS USUALLY MORE WORK AND SOMEWHAT LESS REWARDING THAN GROW-BOXES OR GREENHOUSE GARDENING BUT IT CAN BE DONE WITH SUCCESS. THE MOST IMPORTANT THING IS THAT YOU ARE SUPPLYING THE PLANTS WITH THE VITAL TRACE ELEMENTS THAT ARE OFTEN LACKING IN ORDINARY SOIL.

CLEAR AND LEVEL THE SURFACE OF YOUR TILLED AREA. REMOVE ANY OBVIOUSLY LARGE ROCKS, CLODS, PROTRUDING ROOTS OR WEEDS.

IF THE SOIL IS VERY SANDY, A ROTOTILLER
CAN BE USED TO MIX IN GROUND BARK, SAWDUST,
PEATMOSS OR OTHER SUCH MATERIALS FOR
BETTER MOISTURE RETENTION. IF THE SOIL
IS CLAY, ADD RIVER SAND TO EQUAL ABOUT
50% OF THE TOTAL MIXTURE. MIX THOROUGHLY
WITH A ROTOTILLER OR SHOVEL. CAUTION—
DO NOT ROTOTILL SOIL THAT IS DRY—
NEITHER WHEN REAL WET!

30"

RAKE AND SMOOTH
THE GROUND FIRST.
THEN, LAY OUT THE
DISTANCES BETWEEN
ROWS, 30 INCHES ON
CENTER (SPACING CAN VARY
FROM 28 TO 34 INCHES). STRETCH STRONG
CORD BETWEEN TWO STAKES TO LAY OUT A
STRAIGHT ROW. THE ENTIRE LENGTH OF
THE ROW SHOULD BE FAIRLY LEVEL TO
ALLOW FOR GOOD WATER FLOW
WITHOUT EROSION.

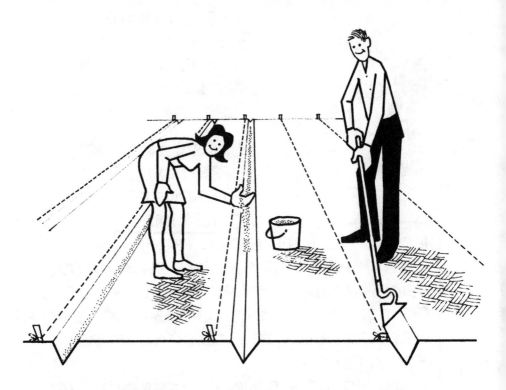

WITH A DIAMOND-POINTED GARDEN TOOL
MAKE A FURROW ABOUT 3-TO 5-INCHES DEEP.
USE THE STRING AS A GUIDE TO KEEP THESE
FURROWS STRAIGHT.

PUT MITTLEIDER'S PRE-PLANT FERTILIZER
MIX INTO THE FURROWS IN THE
FOLLOWING MANNER:

a) SPREAD A NARROW BAND OF THE <u>DRY</u>
PRE-PLANT FERTILIZER MIX BY HAND
DOWN EACH OF THE FURROWS.

b) USE 12 OUNCES OF THE DRY, BLENDED
MIX FOR EVERY <u>10</u> FEET OF FURROW
ROW LENGTH.

c) THEN, SPREAD OVER THE <u>TOP</u> OF THE
FERTILIZER A NARROW BAND OF
LIME.

USE ½-POUND
(8 OUNCES) OF LIME
FOR EACH 10 FEET
OF FURROW ROW
LENGTH.

d) **NOTE**: DO NOT
PRE-MIX THE
FERTILIZER WITH
THE LIME.

HERE IS THE MITTLEIDER PRE-PLANT
FERTILIZER MIXTURE YOU SHOULD USE.
WEIGH CAREFULLY AND MIX THOROUGHLY
THE FOLLOWING -DRY (ENOUGH FOR ¼-ACRE-
VARY ACCORDING TO SIZE OF YOUR PLOT.
SEE APPENDIX III).

    125-POUNDS DOUBLE SUPERPHOSPHATE.
    75-POUNDS POTASSIUM SULFATE OR
        CHLORIDE.
    75-POUNDS SULFATE OF AMMONIA.
    50-POUNDS MAGNESIUM SULFATE.
    5-POUNDS BORON (SODIUM BORATE
        OR BORIC ACID)

APPLIED SEPARATELY:

200-POUNDS OF LIME. USE GYPSUM
LIME FOR DRY CLIMATE. USE
AGRICULTURAL LIME OR DOLOMITE
LIME FOR WET CLIMATE.

    REMEMBER-THESE AMOUNTS ARE
ENOUGH FOR ¼-ACRE, THAT'S 10,000
SQUARE FEET. APPLY AS PREVIOUSLY
DIRECTED, WHETHER THE FURROW ROW
SPACINGS ARE 28,30,OR 34 INCHES ON
CENTER.

e) IF THE SOIL IS DRYING GIVE THE ENTIRE
   SURFACE A LIGHT SPRINKLING WITH WATER
   BEFORE COVERING THE FERTILIZERS IN THE
   FURROW ROWS WITH SOIL.

NOTE: DO <u>NOT</u> COVER FERTILIZERS WITH
<u>DRY SOIL</u> IF PLANTING SEEDS OR
TRANSPLANTING PLANTS.

f) COVER THE
   FERTILIZER BY RAKING
   SOIL OVER IT FROM BETWEEN THE FURROW
   ROWS. RAKE UP ENOUGH SOIL TO MAKE A
   2-TO 3-INCH RAISED RIDGE OVER THE LENGTH
   OF THE FERTILIZER IN THE FURROW ROW.
   THIS BURIES THE FERTILIZER 5 TO 8 INCHES
   BELOW THE TOP OF
   THE RIDGE. THIS IS
   WELL BELOW THE
   EARLY, TENDER
   ROOTS OF
   PLANTS.

g) IF TRANSPLANTING SEE THAT THE ROOTS
   ARE NO CLOSER THAN ABOUT 3 INCHES
   TO THE FERTILIZER IN THE FURROW ROW
   UNDER THE RIDGE.

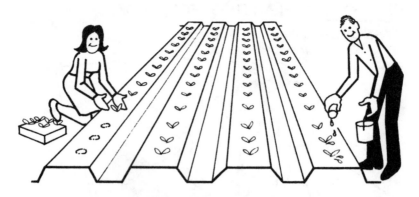

h) PROTECT NEWLY TRANSPLANTED PLANTS OR
   SEED FROM SOIL MAGGOTS, FUNGUS
   DISEASES, CUTWORMS, SLUGS AND SNAILS
   BY APPLYING A PLANTING DRENCH
   IMMEDIATELY <u>AFTER</u> TRANSPLANTING OR
   SEEDING.

HERE IS THE MITTLEIDER PLANTING
DRENCH FORMULA FOR OPEN FURROW
FARMING OR GARDENING.
  55-GALLONS OF WATER
  12-OUNCES CAPTAN (DITHANE OR
       SIMILAR PRODUCTS ARE ALL
       RIGHT).
  4-OUNCES DIAZINON OR SIMILAR
       PRODUCT.

MIX THOROUGHLY TOGETHER AND APPLY
AT THE RATE OF <u>ONE GALLON</u> TO EACH
<u>16 FEET</u> OF FURROW ROW LENGTH.

APPLY DOWN THE PLANT OR SEED ROW <u>ONLY</u>.
<u>DO NOT</u> APPLY IN THE WATER FURROWS
BETWEEN THE RIDGES. CUTWORMS WILL
BE MOST ACTIVE THE FIRST NIGHT AFTER
TRANSPLANTING. CONTROL THEM BY
PLACING 2 OR 3 POISON PELLETS OR A
LARGE PINCH OF POISON BRAN BESIDE
<u>EACH PLANT STEM</u> – <u>AFTER</u> THE WATERING
AND DRENCHING PROCEDURES ABOVE.
SNAILS AND SLUGS CAN BE TAKEN CARE
OF WITH POISONED BAIT AVAILABLE AT
MOST STORES.

i) WATER THE ROWS OF PLANTS BY ALLOWING
WATER FROM A GARDEN HOSE TO MOVE
SLOWLY DOWN THE FURROW LONG
ENOUGH FOR WATER TO <u>SEEP</u> UP INTO
THE RIDGES TO THE PLANT ROOTS.
ONE SUCH WATERING A WEEK IS USUALLY
ENOUGH EVEN IN HOT, ARID AREAS – UNLESS
THE SOIL IS VERY SANDY. WEEDING IS
MINIMIZED BY THIS METHOD OF WATERING.
ONLY THE WATER FURROWS GET WET
ENOUGH FOR WEED SEED TO SPROUT.
ANY KIND OF OVERHEAD SPRINKLING
METHODS WAKE UP WEED SEEDS OVER
THE ENTIRE GARDEN AREA.

j) FEED YOUR PLANTS THE MITTLEIDER
NUTRIENT MIXTURE (CHAPTER 7) FOR
THE FIRST TIME ABOUT THREE WEEKS
AFTER TRANSPLANTING. (REMEMBER THAT
YOU ARE ALREADY WATERING THOROUGHLY
EVERY WEEK – OR AS THE PLANTS REQUIRE.)

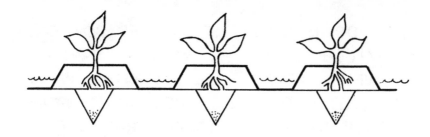

HERE AGAIN FOR YOUR CONVENIENCE IS
THE MITTLEIDER NUTRIENT MIXTURE.
MIX THE FOLLOWING TOGETHER DRY:
  9-POUNDS CALCIUM NITRATE.
  4-POUNDS AMMONIUM NITRATE.
  1½-POUNDS DIAMMONIUM PHOSPHATE.
  4½-POUNDS POTASSIUM SULFATE
      OR CHLORIDE.
  6-POUNDS MAGNESIUM SULFATE
      (EPSOM SALT).
  12-GRAMS BORON (SODIUM BORATE
      OR BORIC ACID)

  4-GRAMS COPPER SULFATE.
  8-GRAMS ZINC SULFATE.
  12-GRAMS MANGANESE SULFATE.
  3-GRAMS MOLYBDIC ACID OR
      SODIUM MOLYBDATE.
  8-OUNCES IRON SULFATE.

NOTE: USUALLY NOT NECESSARY BEFORE
THIRD YEAR OF HEAVY GARDENING. THIS
FORMULA IS USED TO FEED GROWING
PLANTS THOUGHOUT THE ENTIRE GROWING
PERIOD IN FIELD, GROW-BOX, OR
GREENHOUSE GARDENING. FOR SOURCES
OF NUTRIENTS, WRITE THE PUBLISHER.

THE FERTILIZER NUTRIENT
MIXTURE IS SPREAD
DRY BY HAND AND
"WATERED-IN"
AFTER
APPLICATION.

APPLICATION RATE: FOR EVERY 10 FEET OF
ROW LENGTH SPREAD BY HAND 6 OUNCES
OF THIS MIXTURE OF NUTRIENTS IN A
NARROW, EVEN BAND DOWN THE CENTER
OF THE WATER FURROW.

PLANTS GROWN IN THE OPEN FURROW OR
FIELD METHOD ARE FED ONCE EVERY
THREE OR FOUR WEEKS ONLY, AND ALWAYS
JUST BEFORE A WATERING. STOP FEEDING
PLANTS ABOUT TWO WEEKS BEFORE
HARVESTING.

IF YOU HAVE A PROBLEM, YOUR LOCAL
AGRICULTURAL DEPARTMENT OFFICERS
WELCOME OPPORTUNITIES TO HELP. THEY
CAN ADVISE MUCH MORE EFFECTIVELY
FOR YOUR SPECIFIC REGION.
SEE APPENDIX III FOR A CHART OF THE
COMMON NUTRITIONAL DEFICIENCIES
AND INSTRUCTIONS FOR CORRECTING
THEM.

The joy of successful gardening! Like the author, examining these choice melons, you can reap abundant harvests every time with the proven methods described in this book. Success is certain because nothing is left to chance!

THE HARVEST

15

NOTHING IS MORE REWARDING THAN PICKING CHOICE, NUTRITIOUS FRUITS AND VEGETABLES THAT YOUR OWN HANDS AND MIND HAVE HELPED NATURE PRODUCE. HARVEST EARLY IN THE MORNING WHEN PRODUCE IS COOL IF POSSIBLE. OTHERWISE LATE IN THE AFTERNOON WILL DO. HARVEST JUST BEFORE COOKING, EATING, OR CANNING. FRESH-PICKED FOOD, AT ITS PEAK OF PERFECTION, IS HARD TO BEAT! IF YOU PLAN TO STORE PRODUCE FOR AWHILE, COOL IT TO 50°F AS QUICKLY AS POSSIBLE (WITHIN AN HOUR AFTER PICKING).

TEMPERATURES LOWER THAN 45°F TEND TO DEHYDRATE AND WILT VEGETABLES.

HERE IS HOW TO TELL WHEN THINGS ARE READY TO PICK:

ZUCCHINI....ANYTIME BEFORE SKIN TOUGHENS.

RADISH....BEFORE CENTER BEGINS TO
        TURN FIBROUS.

GREEN BUSH OR POLE BEANS....WHEN POD
        IS WELL-FILLED AND SWOLLEN
        BUT BEFORE STRINGS DEVELOP.

BEETS, CELERY, OR CHILI PEPPERS....
        PERSONAL TASTE AS TO SIZE.

CABBAGE....WHEN HEADS ARE SOLID AND
        STILL FIRM.

CHIVES AND PARSLEY....ANYTIME.

CAULIFLOWER AND BROCCOLI....JUST BEFORE
        HEADS BEGIN TO LOOSEN AND
        FLOWER.

SWISS CHARD AND SPINACH....WHILE
        LEAVES ARE STILL TENDER.

CUCUMBER....BEFORE SEEDS DEVELOP.

GREEN ONIONS....WHILE TOPS ARE STILL
        FULL AND CRISP.

DRY ONIONS....AFTER TOPS HAVE DRIED.

SWEET PEPPERS....ANYTIME, THEY ARE
        SWEET EVEN WHEN RED.

EGGPLANT....BEFORE SEEDS ARE
        WELL-DEVELOPED.

TURNIPS....ANY SIZE; USE TOPS LIKE SPINACH.

CANTELOUPE....WHEN THE STEM
        SEPARATES EASILY.

POTATOES....NEW POTATOES (SKIN SLIPS).
        ANYTIME FOR IMMEDIATE USE;
        MATURE ONES AFTER VINES
        BEGIN TO DIE AND SKIN IS TIGHT.

PHOTOGRAPHS

How simple can a greenhouse be! Here is a standard Mittleider grow-box, large enough for all the fresh vegetables you could want, covered with a simple plastic shelter.

The sides of your simple "greenhouse" can be rolled up on pleasant days for ventilation and for easy working of crops, from the sides.

A standard Mittleider greenhouse, simple and inexpensive, provides room for these three grow-boxes, filled with easy-to-work "custom-made soil." See Chapter 10.

Complete economic self-sufficiency, if you wish, on less than half on acre! Food to eat and food to sell for your financial needs. Lush vegetable crops, melons, potatoes, tomatoes — whatever meets your needs or finds a market!

Simple, hand labor can outperform expensive equipment — the Mittleider way! Even for large-scale gardening operations a small rototiller is all the equipment you should ever need. Below: Simple, plastic framework provides for covering shelter if needed.

Tall-growing plants are supported on strings as described in Chapter 8, Page 75.

Tomato vine is pruned of unneeded side growth, leaving flower and fruit-bearing growth (at top).

Four Mittleider grow-boxes, easy to make, easy to work, will provide more than enough food for a large family — in a backyard space. These boxes are filled with soft, mulch-like "custom-made soil" (Chapter 4, Page 45), ready for planting an attractive garden (Chapters 5, 6).

Simple grow-boxes and simple, plastic greenhouse shelter will outperform the largest commercial greenhouse operations at a small fraction of the expense. Average people can do extraordinary gardening with simple, hand tools — with certain success!

Grow-boxes can be purchased in four-foot increments or, as here, simply constructed by leveling and staking boards in place to hold sand-sawdust-nutrient mixture of your choice. See Chapters 2, 3, 4 for detailed drawings and instructions.

Simple Mittleider greenhouse takes shape. Grow-boxes in place; plastic pipe is going on to support covering.

With two layers of plastic covering, you can keep plants growing through cold, cold weather, for out-of-season crops!

Detail showing framework for second layer of plastic, all ready to be covered. (See Chapters 10, 12.)

APPENDICES

APPENDIX - I
QUESTIONS OFTEN ASKED

In seed-starting boxes, can you mix seed varieties?

Generally speaking, yes! If sowed in rows and if the germination periods are similar, several varieties can be seeded in the same box.

Can all varieties of plants be grown in the same area?

Yes and no! Vining plants can smother out low-growing plants, and tall-growing plants can spoil low-growing plants by shading them.

Why do you use redwood or cedar to build grow-boxes?

Only because these woods last much longer. You can use other kinds if you don't mind rebuilding about every second year.

Should the outdoor grow-box face north and south?

This is the preferred direction but it is not imperative.

Can grow-boxes be used for commercial gardening?

Certainly! A small seed-starting house and multiple grow-boxes, with cold-weather protection, can easily make you economically self-sufficient.

Can citrus fruits be grown in a greenhouse in a very cold climate?

Yes, but the economics of it says, "No"!

What is the difference between chemical and mineral fertilizers?

Mainly, the words. If the word minerals were used in both cases there could be no argument.

Are the nutrients you use organic or synthetic?

With the exception of nitrogen they are neither. They are the same as those found in mineral soils.

Is the dry, pre-plant fertilizer mix figured on square feet or cubic feet?

On square feet — whether in the open field, the grow-box, or the greenhouse.

Do fertilizers mixed with water deteriorate rapidly?

No. They may become concentrated when the water evaporates, however, and they are corrosive.

Can the complete nutrient formula be used on berries and trees?

Yes!

How do you control tomato worms?

Control the butterflies that lay the eggs that become the worms.

What makes the flowers on tomato vines fall off?

Lack of water, nitrogen deficiencies, nematodes, nutritional deficiencies, not enough light, fungus, and diseases.

Can white flies in the house or greenhouse be controlled?

Yes, by spraying with the materials available at your supply house.

Why does the fruit of apricot trees turn brown or black at the pit?

Insufficient water, excessive heat two weeks before fruit ripens, boron or calcium deficiency.

What should be done about nematodes?

Sterilize the soil or use the right chemicals to destroy them. See your local agriculture officer.

Should sawdust be pretreated with nitrogen?

If you want to, yes. It is not necessary.

Is it necessary to compost fresh sawdust before using?

No, it can be used right from the saw.

Can mushroom compost be used in place of sawdust?

No! In grow-boxes it can be used as a supplement but not to replace sawdust because it breaks down too quickly.

Are wood ashes good to use as a soil supplement?

They are valuable as a covering over seeds. They are sterilized and have nutritional values.

Are soil-test kits practical?

No! For adequate analysis of soil in the open furrow garden, you need the services of a good laboratory. Ask your local agriculture officer or department.

Can waste materials from the garden be used in soil?

In field gardening they can be worked into the soil where they will decompose.

What can be done to make up for nitrogen shortages?

Use nitrogen fertilizers. If unavailable, bury organic material.

APPENDIX - II
MITTLEIDER
FERTILIZER FORMULAS

These formulas are the result of more than thirty years of testing and successful food production all over the world. They are of immense value to anyone who wishes to greatly increase garden or farm yields.

The materials listed may be available at your farm, garden, or hydroponics supply house. You may also write to J. R. Mittleider, in care of the publisher, for a free listing of the current best sources of ready-mixed materials.

Be sure to read labels and follow instructions when using any concentrated materials — a rule as important in the garden as in the kitchen or workshop. Keep such materials out of reach of children and pets.

PRE-PLANT FERTILIZER FORMULAS

For mixing with your choice of "soil materials" in Mittleider Grow-Boxes (Chapter 4), before planting.

A. **For Grow-Boxes in the standard 8'x30'x10' Mittleider Green-house.**

There are three grow-boxes inside this greenhouse — one on each side, 15 inches wide by 30 feet long; and one in the center, 30 inches wide by 26 feet long (Chapter 9).

173

1. *Before anything else is placed in the grow-boxes, spread two pounds of gypsum evenly* over the original ground (surface) inside the frame of each 15-inch-wide box; three pounds over the inside area of each 30-inch center box.

   (In arid areas, less than 18 inches of rainfall annually, gypsum is preferred; in areas with more than 20 inches of rainfall, agricultural lime or dolomite lime are preferred. In any case, the lime must not be omitted or plants will suffer.)

2. Fill the greenhouse grow-boxes with the inert/organic "soil" materials you have selected (Chapter 4). Make the boxes exactly level-full, without tamping down.

3. Spread evenly, right on top of the "soil materials," the following formula for each 15-inch by 30-foot box:

   1 pound double superphosphate
   ½ pound potassium sulfate or chloride
   1 pound sulfate of ammonia
   ½ pound magnesium sulfate (Epsom salt)
   ½ **ounce** boron (sodium borate or boric acid)

Spread separately:

   1 pound, **4 ounces** lime (gypsum), or agricultural lime — (See 1 above).

   For each center box, 30 inches by 26 feet, nearly double the above formula.

4. Thoroughly mix the above fertilizers and the inert/organic "soil materials." Again level the materials in the box.

B. **For Mittleider 5'x30'x8" Outdoor Grow-Boxes**

1. Spread 10 pounds of gypsum over the inside floor area, right on the original soil (surface), inside each 5-foot by 30-foot by 8-inch box. (See note on rainfall and lime-choice in A-1 above.)

2. Fill the grow-boxes with the inert/organic "soil materials (Chapter 4), then spread this formula over the top:

   4 pounds double superphosphate
   4 pounds sulfate of ammonia
   2 pounds potassium sulfate or chloride
   2 pounds magnesium sulfate (Epsom salt)
   2 **ounces** boron (sodium borate or boric acid)

Spread separately:

   5 pounds lime (See note on rainfall and
lime-choice in A-1 above.)

PLANT-FEEDING NUTRIENT MIX

To feed growing plants throughout the entire growing cycle, whether in outdoor grow-boxes, greenhouses, or open field. (See Chapter 7 for method of application.)

Weigh accurately and mix very thoroughly together (dry):

   9 pounds calcium nitrate
   4 pounds ammonium nitrate
   1½ pounds diammonium phosphate (21-53-0)
   4½ pounds potassium sulfate or chloride
   6 pounds magnesium sulfate (Epsom salt)
   8 **ounces** iron sulfate
   *4 **grams** copper sulfate
   *8 **grams** zinc sulfate
   *12 **grams** manganese sulfate
   12 **grams** boron (sodium borate or boric acid)
   *3 **grams** molybdenum (sodium molybdate or
   molybdic acid)

*Include these for the complete mixture for greenhouse grow-boxes — always; for outdoor grow-boxes or open field, use only if visual symptoms or soil test indicate need.

This mixture is applied by hand as dry granules (Chapter 7).

This formula contains all the essential foods plants must have to be healthy. Eacr separate compound contains water molecules and they can be mixed together, but when mixed together, the formula will dissolve into a sticky solution after 5-10 days. This does not affect the potency but makes it very hard to apply the material as a fertilizer.

OPTIONAL PLANT-FEEDING NUTRIENT MIXTURE

If the complete nutrient formula above is unavailable, substitute the following formula for outdoor crops, applying at the same rate as the regular formula. (Greenhouse crops will fail if the complete nutrient mixture above is not used.)

Weigh carefully and mix thoroughly together (dry):

> 8 pounds ammonium nitrate
> 6 pounds magnesium sulfate (Epsom salt)
> 1½ pounds diammonium phosphate (21-53-0)
> 4½ pounds potassium sulfate or chloride
> 10 **grams** boron (sodium borate or boric acid)

Note: the complete formula above and this substitute formula are for feeding *growing* plants — not to take the place of the pre-plant fertilizers. This optional formula will probably produce well for two or three years before the crops decline due to trace-mineral deficiencies (See Appendix III). The soil cannot produce beyond its most limiting factor.

SEEDLING NUTRIENT SOLUTION

This is a formula for the "seedhouse" — used to feed all *sprouted* seeds and seedlings in the seedhouse, regardless of plant size — until they are set out as transplants. This formula is used as a constant feed, meaning that every watering of the plants is with this solution. Note that before seeds sprout, only *water* is used to keep them moist.

Measure accurately and mix together:

> 55 gallons water (1 drum)
> 8 ounces ammonium nitrate
> 2 ounces magnesium sulfate
> 2 ounces potassium sulfate or chloride
> 2 ounces diammonium phosphate

Or:

> 3 gallons water
> 13 **grams** ammonium nitrate
> 3 **grams** magnesium sulfate
> 3 **grams** potassium sulfate or chloride
> 3 **grams** diammonium phosphate (21-53-0)

TRANSPLANTING FORMULA

This formula is for feeding and minimizing transplanting shock when plants are transplanted to where they will mature — in grow-boxes, in the greenhouse, or in the open furrow field. This operation is done just once, at the time of transplanting (Chapter 6).

Give each plant 1 pint of this solution (makes enough for 440 plants):

> 55 gallons water
> 2 pounds ammonium nitrate
> 1 pound diammonium phosphate (21-53-0)
> 8 **ounces** potassium sulfate or chloride
> 8 **ounces** magnesium sulfate (Epsom salt)

If local conditions indicate need, add:

> 4 **ounces** Diazinon (or similar product
>   for soil maggot control)
> 12 **ounces** Dithane-45, Benlate (or similar product
>   for control of fungus)

PRE-PLANT FERTILIZER FORMULA
FOR OPEN-FURROW GARDEN OR FARM

Formula to be spread in a narrow band and covered carefully with soil before planting seeds or plants. See Chapter 14 for method of application.

For 1 acre —

> 500 pounds double superphosphate
> 300 pounds potassium sulfate or chloride
> 300 pounds sulfate of ammonia
> 200 pounds magnesium sulfate
> 20 pounds boron (sodium borate or boric acid)

Applied separately before mixing the above with the soil:

> 800 pounds lime (in arid areas — less than 18 inches rainfall — gypsum is preferred; in areas with more than 20 inches rainfall, agricultural lime or dolomite lime is preferred.)

For ¼ acre — 10,000 square feet:

> 125 pounds double superphosphate
> 75 pounds potassium sulfate or chloride
> 75 pounds sulfate of ammonia
> 50 pounds magnesium sulfate (Epsom salt)
> 5 pounds boron (sodium borate or boric acid)

Applied separately:

> 200 pounds lime (See above)

Per 100 lineal feet of plant row length:

> 2 pounds, 12 ounces double superphosphate
> 1 pound, 12 ounces potassium sulfate or chloride
> 1 pound, 12 ounces sulfate of ammonia
> 1 pound, 4 ounces magnesium sulfate
> 24 **grams** boron

Apply separately:

> 2 pounds lime (See above)

Per 10 lineal feet of plant row length:

> 4½ ounces double superphosphate
> 84 grams potassium sulfate or chloride
> 84 grams sulfate of ammonia
> 60 grams magnesium sulfate
> 6 grams boron

Apply separately:

> 4 ounces lime (See above)

Notes: There are 175 rows of plants in 1 acre — if the rows are 100 feet long and spaced 30 inches apart.

Weights are figured on the basis of 30 grams per ounce; 16 ounces per pound.

UNITS OF MEASURE

60 drops	=	1 teaspoon
3 teaspoons	=	1 tablespoon
1 tablespoon	=	½ ounce
16 tablespoons	=	1 cup
1 cup	=	8 ounces
16 fluid ounces	=	2 cups
2 cups	=	1 pint
½ liquid pint	=	1 cup
2 pints	=	1 quart
4 quarts	=	1 gallon
1 pound	=	16 ounces
1 pint	=	1 pound
1 gallon	=	8.337 pounds (8 pounds)
1 mile	=	5,280 ft., or 320 rods
1 acre	=	43,560 square feet
		or 160 square rods

To Change Centigrade to Fahrenheit

Multiply centigrade by 9/5 and add 32 degrees

To Change Fahrenheit to Centigrade

Subtract 32 degrees and multiply by 5/9.

Equivalent Rates in Applying Fertilizers

1 ounce per square foot = 2,722.5 pounds per acre
1 ounce per square yard = 302.5 pounds per acre
1 ounce per 100 square feet = 27.2 pounds per acre
1 pound per 1,000 sq. ft. = 43.6 pounds per acre

1 pound per acre = 1/3 ounce per 1,000 sq. ft.
5 gallons per acre = 1 pint per 1,000 sq. ft.
100 gallons per acre = 2½ gallons per 1,000 sq. ft.
100 gallons per acre = 20 pounds per 1,000 sq. ft.
100 gallons per acre = 1 quart per 100 sq. ft.

FERTILIZER FORMULAS
FOR SPECIAL-SIZE GROW-BOXES
(4' Square Segments)

PRE-PLANT FERTILIZER

4'x4'x8" Grow-Boxes
> 6½ ounces double superphosphate
> 3¼ ounces potassium sulfate or chloride
> 6½ ounces sulfate of ammonia
> 3¼ ounces magnesium sulfate (Epsom salt)
> 6 **grams** boron (sodium borate or boric acid)
> 1½ pounds lime*

4'x8'x8" Grow-Boxes
> 13 ounces double superphosphate
> 6½ ounces potassium sulfate or chloride
> 13 ounces sulfate of ammonia
> 6½ ounces magnesium sulfate
> 12 **grams** boron (sodium borate or boric acid)
> 3 pounds lime*

4'x12'x8" Grow-Boxes

1¼ pounds double superphosphate
10 **ounces** potassium sulfate or chloride
1¼ pounds sulfate of ammonia
10 **ounces** magnesium sulfate
18 **grams** boron
4½ pounds lime*

4'x16'x8" Grow-Boxes

1 pound, 10 ounces double superphosphate
13 ounces potassium sulfate or chloride
1 pound, 10 ounces sulfate of ammonia
13 ounces magnesium sulfate
24 **grams** boron
6 pounds lime*

4'x20'x8" Grow-Boxes

2 pounds double superphosphate
1 pound potassium sulfate or chloride
2 pounds sulfate of ammonia
1 pound magnesium sulfate
1 **ounce** boron
7½ pounds lime

4'x24'x8" Grow-Boxes

2 pounds, 8 ounces double superphosphate
1 pound, 4 ounces potassium sulfate or chloride
2 pounds, 8 ounces sulfate of ammonia
1 pound, 4 ounces magnesium sulfate
36 **grams** boron
9 pounds lime*

*In selecting the type of lime to use follow the instructions given previously for the standard size grow-boxes.

PLANT FEEDING NUTRIENT MIX

4'x4'x8" Grow-Boxes
64 grams (2 ounces)

4'x8'x8" Grow-Boxes
128 grams (4¼ ounces)

4'x12'x8" Grow-Boxes
192 grams (6½ ounces)

4'x16'x8" Grow-Boxes
256 grams (8½ ounces)

4'x20'x8" Grow-Boxes
320 grams (11 ounces)

4'x24'x8" Grow-Boxes
384 grams (13 ounces)

Note: Apply the fertilizers and water as outlined for the standard size grow-boxes.

APPENDIX - III

PLANT NUTRIENT DEFICIENCIES

Here are the nutrients plants require for growth. Deficiencies of the first eight most commonly produce nutritional problems.

1. Nitrogen
2. Phosphorous
3. Potassium
4. Magnesium
5. Calcium
6. Iron
7. Boron
8. Molybdenum
9. Manganese
10. Copper
11. Zinc
12. Sulfur
13. Chlorine

NUTRITIONAL DEFICIENCY
SYMPTOMS AND CORRECTIONS

The amounts of nutrients/fertilizers recommended here are based on:

1. The standard Mittleider greenhouse (8'x30') containing three grow-boxes — two, 15"x30' (one on each side); and one, 30"x26' in the center. The amount shown in each case is for one 15"x30' box and should be nearly doubled for the 30"x26' box.

2. The standard Mittleider outdoor grow-box (5'x30').

   Nutrients indicated should be spread evenly over the entire box area. See additional instructions for application at the end of this Appendix.

Nitrogen Deficiency

SYMPTOMS: general yellowing over entire plant; spindly, stunted growth.

CORRECTION:
1. **greenhouse** grow-box — 1 pound, 12 ounces ammonium nitrate.
2. **outdoor** grow-box — 2 pounds ammonium nitrate.

Phosphorous Deficiency

SYMPTOMS: a purplish discoloration of older leaves; stunted growth, poor fruit set.

CORRECTION:
1. **greenhouse** grow-box — 12 ounces diammonium phosphate.
2. **outdoor** grow-box — 1 pound diammonium phosphate.

Potassium Deficiency

SYMPTOMS: scorching ("firing") of edges of mature leaves; shriveled seeds in cereal crops; poor fruit quality.

CORRECTION:
1. **greenhouse** grow-box — 1 pound potassium sulfate or chloride.
2. **outdoor** grow-box — 1 pound, 8 ounces potassium sulfate or chloride.

Magnesium Deficiency

SYMPTOMS: older leaves have dead areas and general yellowing; abnormally bright colors in older leaves — bright reds, oranges, yellows.

CORRECTION:
1. **greenhouse** grow-box — 2 pounds magnesium sulfate.
2. **outdoor** grow-boxes — 2 pounds, 12 ounces magnesium sulfate.

Calcium Deficiency

SYMPTOMS: dead terminal buds; stunted root growth.

CORRECTION:
1. **greenhouse** grow-box — 1 pound, 8 ounces calcium nitrate.
2. **outdoor** grow-box — 1 pound, 12 ounces calcium nitrate.

Iron Deficiency

SYMPTOMS: yellowing of terminal buds with leaf veins remaining green.

CORRECTION:
1. **greenhouse** grow-box — 1 pound iron sulfate.
1. **outdoor** grow-box — 1 pound, 4 ounces iron sulfate.

Boron Deficiency

SYMPTOMS: death of terminal buds; black heart of tubers; flower end-rot of tomatoes.

CORRECTION:
1. **greenhouse** grow-box — 36 **grams** (1¼ ounces) boron, as sodium borate or boric acid, mixed with 1 cup sawdust or sand.
2. **outdoor** grow-box — 60 **grams** (2 ounces) boron, as sodium borate or boric acid, mixed with 3 quarts sawdust or sand.

Molybdenum Deficiency

SYMPTOMS: "whiptail disease" (see Color Plates), narrow, long leaves, producing twisting patterns.

CORRECTION:
1. **greenhouse** grow-box — 8 **grams** (less than half an ounce) sodium molybdate or molybdic acid, mixed in 1 cup sawdust or sand.
2. **outdoor** grow-box — 16 **grams** sodium molybdate or molybdic acid, mixed in 1 cup sawdust or sand.

When a deficiency symptom is spotted, corrective measures should be taken as quickly as possible. For example: assume that the grow-box has just been fertilized with the regular plant-feeding nutrient mix and watered. A deficiency symptom is spotted and diagnosed. Do not attempt correction on the same day as a regular feeding and watering but don't wait a week either. The next day after spotting the symptom, apply the corrective nutrient (as dry material spread evenly over the box area) and water again with the regular amount of water. Do not repeat the corrective application until several weeks have elapsed.

Note that a deficiency correction is in addition to the regular feeding program, not along with it. In other words, don't simply add the corrective nutrient to your regular feeding mixture; make a separate application, followed by a separate watering.

APPENDIX - IV

MATERIALS LISTS FOR GROW-BOXES AND GREENHOUSES

STANDARD MITTLEIDER OUTDOOR GROW-BOX
(5'x30'x8")
(See drawings, Chapter 3)

Wood

70 feet 1"x8"x20' redwood (or cedar) lumber
25 1"x2"x18" pointed redwood stakes

Other Materials

1 pound blue shingle nails
1 pound 4-inch box nails

Tools

1 3-pound mall or hammer
1 regular-weight hammer
1 level, two feet or longer
100 feet strong cord

MATERIALS TO CONVERT A STANDARD OUTDOOR GROW-BOX INTO A SIMPLE GREENHOUSE

(See drawings, Chapter 9)

A. Box covered with one layer of plastic cover

Wood
90 feet 1"x2" boards, 20' lengths if possible

Plastic
152 feet ¾" PVC pipe, lightweight (200PST)
20 feet 1" PVC pipe, lightweight (200PST)
16 ¾" PVC T-joints
16 ¾" PVC 45° elbows
1 pint plastic cement
50 feet 4 mil, 16-foot-wide clear plastic

Cut plastic pipe to these lengths:

¾" PVC pipe: 8 pieces, 60" long — for the width.
16 pieces, 48" long — for the legs.
8 pieces, 72" long — for the arched roof.
1" PVC pipe: 15 pieces, 15" long — base for legs.

Other Materials
1" metal 'U" clamps
60 feet ordinary bailing wire
½ pound 2-inch galvanized nails

B. Materials for second plastic layer in colder climates

Wood
210 feet 1"x2" boards, 20' lengths if possible

Plastic
140 feet ¾" PVC pipe, lightweight (200PST)
20 feet 1" PVC pipe, lightweight (200PST)
4 ¾" PVC T-joints
16 ¾" PVC 45° elbows
50 feet, 4 mil, 16-foot-wide clear plastic

Cut plastic pipe to these lengths:

¾" PVC pipe: 2 pieces, 64" long — for the width
16 pieces, 56" long — for the legs
8 pieces, 76" long — for the arched roof
1" PVC pipe: 15 pieces, 15" long — base for legs

Other Materials
50 feet ordinary bailing wire
1 quart white exterior paint
1 pound 2-inch box nails

Note: This list of materials does not include those needed for making doors on both ends of this type of greenhouse, nor an extra 60' of 1"x8" boards needed to divide the grow-box, leaving an aisle down the center. See Chapter 10 for illustrations.

STANDARD MITTLEIDER GREENHOUSE (8'x30'x10')
(See drawings, Chapter 10)

A. Materials for frame, grow-boxes, and one layer of plastic cover

Wood
60 feet 2"x6" boards, 10' or 20' lengths
4 2"x6" boards, 8' length
280 feet 1"x2" boards, 10' or 20' lengths
8 2"x2" boards, 12' length
8 2"x2" boards, 6' length
200 feet 1"x8" boards, 10' or 20' lengths
4 2"x4" boards, 8' length
8 4"x4" posts, 9' long
50 1"x2"x18" pointed redwood stakes
1 bundle lath

Plastic
260 feet ¾" PVC pipe, lightweight (200 PST), 20' lengths
20 feet 1" PVC pipe, lightweight (200 PST), 20' length
16 ¾" PVC T-joints
16 ¾" PVC 45° elbows
50 feet 2 or 4 mil clear plastic, 16' width
1 pint plastic cement

Cut plastic pipe to these lengths:

¾" PVC pipe: 8 pieces, 96" long — for the width
16 pieces, 82" long — for the legs
8 pieces, 108" long — for the arched roof
1" PVC pipe: 16 pieces, 15" long — base for legs

Other Materials
1 pound blue lath nails
2 pounds 4-inch box nails
2 pounds 3-inch box nails
2 pounds 6-inch box nails
4 "D" shaped door hinges, 3
180 feet No. 2 wire
12 ⅜"x6" eye bolts, threaded
16 1" metal "U" clamps
60 ¾" metal "U" clamps
3 quarts white exterior paint

B. Materials for second layer of plastic in colder climates

Wood
30 feet 2"x2" boards, 10' lengths
180 feet 1"x2" boards, 10' or 20' lengths
1 bundle lath

Plastic
220 feet ¾" PVC pipe, lightweight (200 PST), 20' lengths
20 feet 1" PVC pipe, lightweight (200 PST), 20' lengths
4 ¾" PVC T-joints
16 ¾" PVC 45° elbows
50 feet 4 mil clear plastic, 16' width
32 feet 4 mil clear plastic, 12" width

Cut plastic pipe to these lengths:

¾" PVC pipe: 2 pieces, 101½" long — for the width
16 pieces, 90" long — for the legs
8 pieces, 114" long — for the arched roof
1" PVC pipe: 15 pieces, 15" long — base for legs

Other Materials
 4 1" metal "U" clamps
 8 ¾" metal "U" clamps
 40 3/16"x4" threaded bolts with nuts
 16 2/16"x2½" threaded bolts with nuts

C. Measurements for three greenhouse grow-boxes

Materials are included above for the three standard grow-boxes in the standard Mittleider greenhouse. Two boxes (either side of greenhouse) are 15" wide by 30' long, outside measurements; one box (center) is 30" wide by 26' long — cut short 24" on both ends of greenhouse to allow for aisle access. See Chapter 10 for detailed illustrations.

APPENDIX - V

COMMERCIAL APPLICATIONS OF THE MITTLEIDER METHOD

Dramatically increased yields — and income — are possible, even on poor land, with the simple 5'x30' grow-boxes and the inexpensive 8'x30' plastic greenhouses described in this book.

The world demand for food increases daily and the problem is growing in intensity!

The so-called "good land" on planet Earth is already under intensive cultivation. But there are still millions of acres of "earth" lying idle in most countries.

Over the years, crop yields per acre on this "good land" have increased many fold, and no doubt will be increased still more. Just how much more remains to be seen. It is reasonable to believe that future increases will be limited in comparison to the recent past.

The greatest hope for providing food for an expanding world population is in the millions of acres of land that today lie unused, unproductive.

Until very recently, this land was regarded as worthless — but today it has been proven that a very large part of this "worthless" land can be used very easily and with maximum results.

Simple grow-boxes, covered where necessary by inexpensive, plastic greenhouses, present the key to agricultural use of this land. Their dramatic productiveness in our Mittleider demonstration projects in many countries is unchallengeable.

Look at the following comparative figures — you will be surprised!

Comparison of grow-box/greenhouse farming with some other types of farming

Crop: CABBAGE

Conventional Tractor Farming

Number of plants per acre	14-15,000
Average weight per head	3 pounds
Marketable heads per acre	40-50%
Marketable cabbage per acre	24,000 pounds
Crop income per acre at 8¢ lb.	$1,920
Possible crops per year	2 (?)
Potential income per acre, per year	$3,840

5'x30'8" Grow-Boxes

Number of plants per grow-box	135
Grow-boxes per acre	156
Plants per acre (135x156	19,000
Average weight per head	3 pounds
Marketable heads per acre	90%
Marketable cabbage per acre	51,300 pounds
Crop income per acre at 8¢ lb.	$4,004
Possible crops per year	2 or 3
Potential income per acre at 2 crops	$8,008

Note: Conventional farming requires heavy mechanization. Grow-box farming, after the small cost of lumber, requires virtually no equipment — just one 7HP rototiller is all the machinery needed. Grow-boxes organize farming so that *hand labor can compete with farm machinery* — and make it possible to use much of the poorest and heretofore unusable land.

Crop: TOMATO

Large, Automated, Hydroponic Greenhouse

Greenhouse size	150'x30' (1/9 acre)
Cost to construct and equip	$25,000
Tomato plants per greenhouse	1,680
Fruit per plant (6-months picking)	10 pounds
Fruit per house, per crop	16,800 pounds
Fruit *per acre* (9 houses)	75 tons
Crop income per house, per crop at 25¢ lb.	$4,200
Crops per year	1½
Crop income per house, per year	$6,300
Income potential per acre per year	$56,700

Simple, 8'x30'x10' Greenhouse

Greenhouses per acre	86
Cost to construct and equip, inc. heat	$385
Tomato plants per greenhouse	150
Fruit per plant (4 months picking)	14-20 pounds
Fruit per house, per crop at 16 lb.	2,400 pounds
Fruit *per acre* (86 houses)	103 tons
Crop income per house, per crop at 25¢ lb.	$600
Crops per year	2
Crop income per house per year	$1,200
Income potential per acre per year	$103,200

Note: Modern hydroponic greenhouses require much equipment and continuous, fixed monthly expenses for operating.

The Mittleider 8'x30' greenhouse (except for the simple heating equipment already included in the $385 construction cost) requires *no* special equipment or machinery to operate. This eliminates the heavy monthly expenses and turns man-hour production into ready cash.

As the figures indicate, there is an improvement in crop yields with the small greenhouse and it allows the use of land formerly considered "worthless."

Other Books by Jacob R. Mittleider:

FOOD FOR EVERYONE

A comprehensive treatment of the Mittleider Method. Sixty-four chapters, 608 pages, and a thousand drawings, photographs, and color plates. Detailed discussion of all aspects of plant growth, soil and water, nutrients, disease and insect control, harvesting and marketing. Large format, hard cover, $30. *Source: Jacob R. Mittleider, 2145 Browning St., Salt Lake City, UT 84108.*

GROW-BED GARDENING

In easy-to-prepare earthen beds, the Mittleider Method produces enormous increases in garden yields for both home gardeners and commercial growers. Precise, easy-to-follow methods for exact fertilization against common nutritional deficiencies. Valuable tips on weed control, easy care of plants, and water conservation—andmore benefits of Mittleider's remarkable system. Nearly 750 photographs illustrate every step. Large format, $14.95.

Source: Woodbridge Press, PO Box 6189, Santa Barbara, CA 93160. 1-800-237-6053.

THE GARDEN DOCTOR

Three-volume set in brilliant color illustrates nutritional deficiencies of plants with hundreds of before-and-after photographs in each volume. Shows the appearance of plants affected with specific deficiencies, describes proper treatment, shows appearance of healthy plants. Plants respond quickly to application of proper nutrients, with greatly increased food production. Large format.

For information call 1-800-323-5100.

LET'S GROW TOMATOES

All about tomatoes, from sprouting seed right through harvesting. It includes cultural methods, pruning, feeding, control of common diseases, how to grow strong seedlings, and how to overcome the problem of cracked fruit. The Grow-Box method to bountiful tomato harvests! $10. *Source: Jacob R. Mittleider, 2145 Browning St., Salt Lake City, UT 84108.*

GARDENING BY THE FOOT

The Mittleider Method at work in narrow garden beds. Illustrates how to plant and nurture various food crops in limited space. Details of bed construction, fertilization, harvesting. *Source: Jacob R. Mittleider, 2145 Browning St., Salt Lake City, UT 84108.*

MITTLEIDER TECHNICAL BULLETINS:

A series of technical bulletins concentrating on special aspects of food production using the Mittleider Method.

$3 each. Entire set $25. Source:
Jacob R. Mittleider, 2145 Browning St., Salt Lake City , UT 84108.

Stock No.
IFPM
1000
SOILS — TYPES AND FUNCTIONS OF SOILS.
A full explanation on how to modify depleted soils to improve crop production.

Stock No.
IFPM
1001
SPROUTING — MORE ON SPROUTING SEEDS AND TRANSPLANTING PLANTS.
A detailed manual devoted to growing healthy seedlings.

Stock No.
IFPM
1002
GREENHOUSES — GREENHOUSE PRODUCTION PROBLEMS AND HOW TO AVOID THEM.
A manual that everyone interested in greenhouse production should have for ready reference.

Stock No.
IFPM
1003
FERTILIZERS — MORE ON FERTILIZER MANAGEMENT
Condensed information on 15 factors that affect crop yield.

Stock No.
IFPM
1004
SYMPTOMS: DEFICIENCY SYMPTOMS.
Describing deficiency symptoms and how to recognize them on various vegetable plants.

Stock No.
IFPM
1005
OSMOSIS: MORE ON FERTILIZERS AND OSMOSIS.
A simple explanation on the process of how plants absorb their nutrients. A very important manual.

Stock No.
IFPM
1006
MANURES — BONUS BENEFITS FROM ANIMAL MANURES.
Unbiased information about animal manures including manure "tea" recipe and how to use it.

Stock No.
IFPM
1007
GROWING VEGETABLES WITHOUT FERTILIZERS.
How to grow vegetables when neither animal manures, compost, or chemical fertilizers are available.

Stock No.
IFPM
1008
FERTILIZERS CONDENSED.
High points grouped for quick reference on all 13 essential nutrients including sodium.